M000201755

OWNING IT

TAKE CONTROL OF YOUR LIFE, WORK, AND CAREER

THE JOYS,
OPPORTUNITIES,
& RISKS OF
BECOMING A
CONSULTANT

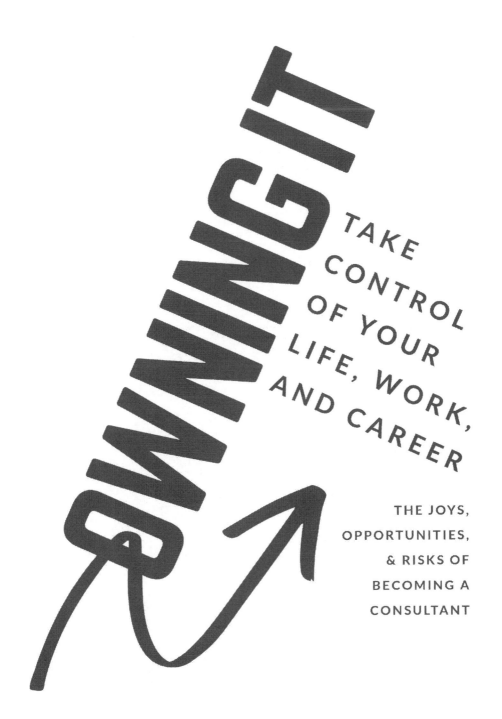

OWNING IT

TAKE CONTROL OF YOUR LIFE, WORK, AND CAREER

THE JOYS, OPPORTUNITIES, & RISKS OF BECOMING A CONSULTANT

KRIS TAYLOR

Niche Pressworks
Indianapolis

Owning It: Take Control of Your Life, Work, and Career
ISBN 978-1-946533-64-7 ebook
ISBN 978-1-946533-65-4 paperback

For permission to reprint portions of this content or bulk purchases, contact Katie McNamee at Explore@LeapRightNow.biz

Published by Niche Pressworks, Indianapolis, IN
http://NichePressworks.com

Printed in the United States of America

DEDICATION

To the independent professionals I work with, day in and day out, who strive to make this world a better place for ourselves, the children in our lives, and the generations to follow.

To my clients, who understand the value we can create together by doing good work in partnership.

ACKNOWLEDGEMENTS

This book would not be possible without a host of others who have shown me the way, who have walked by my side, and who have encouraged me when I was down, have taught me when I was clueless, and have been role models for me about how to walk in this world with integrity, passion, and purpose.

Thanks to my Evergreen Leadership Practice Partners, who help me deliver successful engagements and enable me to grow by sharing their wisdom.

I offer my deep gratitude to my clients, who with every engagement, open new possibilities in collaborative partnerships.

A special thanks to Katie McNamee, my partner in LEAP, who continually teaches me about measured risk-taking and common sense strategy execution.

And finally, with great gratitude to Nicole Gebhardt and Kim Han at Niche Pressworks, who made the daunting task of publishing this book doable.

CONTENTS

CONTENTS

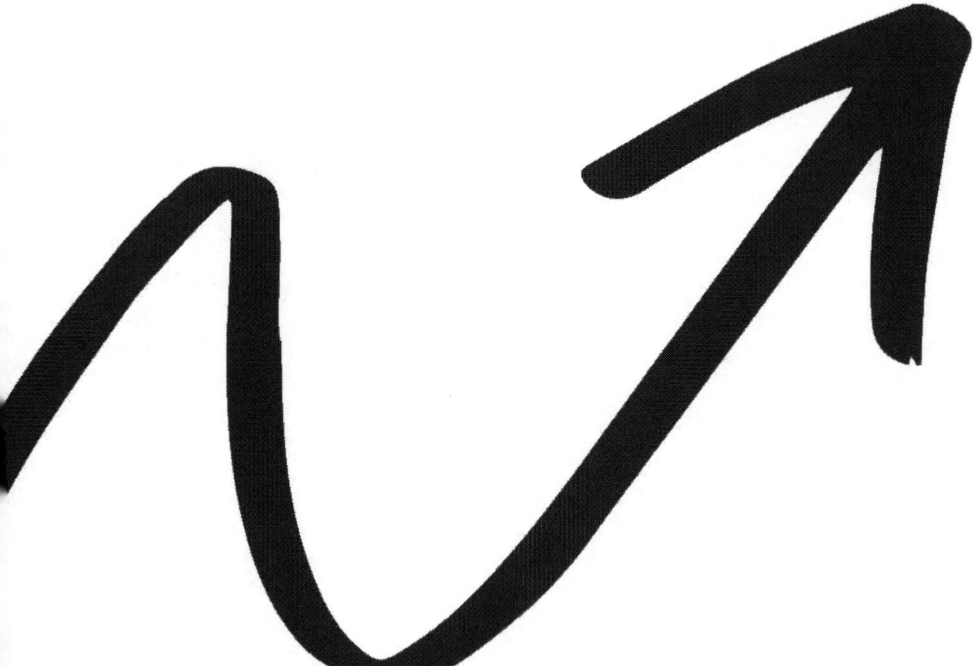

PREFACE

MY TWISTY CAREER

If I had only one word to describe my career, it would be twisty. And it was very, very twisty for the first 25 years until I began to own it. Now my career still has a few gentle turns, but the radical shifts I made earlier are gone. My career path is straighter and heading toward a wonderful place while I enjoy every step of the way!

I started with a decade in nonprofit, working first for others and then starting a nonprofit organization. That was followed by fourteen years at RR Donnelley, a Fortune 200 company, where I had eight roles across five functions and in three very different environments: assisting with a greenfield start-up, HR and operations roles in the company's oldest manufacturing plant, and then a corporate role in learning and development. I went out on my own at the age of 50, founding two consulting practices, and teaching entrepreneurship classes.

All that twistiness, while at times confusing and frustrating (would I NEVER find the career that suited me best?), turned out to be pure gold. The lessons I learned serve me every day. The relationships I made were rich and broad. And I learned how to reinvent myself and the workplaces where I've been lucky enough to serve.

By owning the twists, I've crafted a career that serves me well and serves my clients well. In 2004, I founded a consulting practice that has evolved into Evergreen Leadership (EvergreenLeadership.com), where we create customized leadership development programs for leaders at all levels. In 2017, Katie McNamee and I cofounded LEAP (LeapRightNow.biz) to help others who wanted to take control of their career and life make the leap from corporate to consulting.

The words I use to describe my current career and life's work would include rich, rewarding, fun, and flexible. At the age of 25 or 35 (or even 45)—I would not have imagined that my career would evolve into this!

I do the work I love, the work I do well, and the work I feel called to do. I have found a way to earn a good income in a career that allows me the flexibility to balance my work and life in ways that a traditional full-time job would not. I am constantly challenged in a good way—one that grows my skills and sharpens my abilities. I can't imagine doing it any other way.

More and more skilled professionals are choosing, just like me, to take their talents and skills into the marketplace as independent consultants and freelancers. In this book, I hope to help those who are considering or who are on the path to independence. Organizations continue to become leaner, more flexible, and more in need of the right skills at the right time. I have some keen insights on how those leading organizations can partner with independent consultants and freelancers in ways that work for both parties.

As I look back, there is one thing that is crystal clear: the workplace I entered in the 1980s looks very different than the workplace of today. And yet, at a foundational level, human beings are still looking for the timeless things that work provides them: a living and a life. Food and shelter. Meaning and purpose. Bread and roses.

For an increasing number of skilled professionals, going independent lets them take control of their career and integrate their life and work in healthy ways. Let me share with you what I've learned about doing this over the past fifteen years.

INTRODUCTION

THE INDEPENDENT PROFESSIONAL

I've been in the workforce for a long time—long enough to see how dramatically and quickly things are changing. Organizations are leaner, meaning fewer people are doing more work. The impact of technology, artificial intelligence (AI), and automation is spreading from the factory floor to professional fields that were considered untouchable a decade ago. Globalization combined with technology means that work can be done anywhere at any time, improving the lives of some and threatening the livelihood of others. The half-life of knowledge is such that by the time a student graduates from college in a technical field, half of what they just learned is already obsolete.

> The impact of technology, artificial intelligence (AI), and automation is spreading from the factory floor to professional fields that were considered untouchable a decade ago.

Professional work is changing as a result. The hot professional jobs of today were unheard of a decade ago. What professionals do now, and increasingly in the future, will be supplemented by AI in ways we could not conceive of a few years ago. But that is not the only thing that is changing—perhaps the most dramatic shift is not in what we do, but how we do it.

1

Generations ago, what you did was likely what your parents did. What they did was likely what their parents did. You farmed or were merchants or seafaring families.

A century ago, the career you started with was quite likely the one you ended with. After your education, the norm was to land a good job with a big company. And you would work there and stay there until retirement.

Today, the career you start with is usually only the first of many. College grads are predicted to have upwards of six careers (or more) in their working life. Not jobs, but careers. And many of those careers will not even exist at college graduation but instead will evolve quickly as technology, globalization, and societies advance.

Not only is what we do changing, but how we do what we do is also changing. Centuries ago, people worked in family units or as small merchants. In the 20th century, most worked as employees. Today, the world of work—in all areas including professional work—is moving towards self-employment.

We call it the gig economy or the freelance nation. You might think this is about Uber drivers or twentysomethings that code or people who rent their homes through Airbnb. Think again.

By 2028, over half of the professional workforce will be independent (Pofeldt 2017), and that includes the professional jobs typically associated with working for a company. Read that last sentence one more time! If you are in accounting, finance, marketing, procurement, HR, IT, sales, engineering, R&D, quality, or any other traditional professional field, you may one day be working as an independent professional rather than an employee. No matter what your profession. No matter where you live. No matter what industry you work in.

This book will help you navigate the emerging landscape of independent professional work. In addition to considering what is changing and why, I share practical advice for professionals, particularly those thinking about or already making a living independently.

After fifteen years of doing this, I have some wisdom on the topic. Much of what I've learned came from master consultants and some from the school of hard knocks. Some I gained from teaching entrepreneurship and consulting at Purdue University and even more from starting two successful independent consulting practices.

Even still, there are three disclaimers I must make:

I am not a perfect prognosticator. I strongly believe that the demand for independent professions will continue to grow. All indicators point in that direction. Yet there are too many factors in play. Each influences the others and make it difficult to know what the future will bring with any degree of exactness.

I speak only to the career implications for skilled professionals with marketable skills. This is the world I know, study, and practice within. The workplace trends discussed in this book WILL impact entry-level and blue-collar and service workers—but this is NOT an area I am qualified to weigh in on.

One size does not fit all. Each professional has unique skills, abilities, interests, demands, passions, goals, and life circumstances. I seek to be descriptive rather than prescriptive; each professional has the opportunity to use these insights and ideas and adapt them in ways that suit them best.

And so, before we start, I want to be clear that I don't have all the answers. This book draws from my work in organizations and with professionals who are carving out careers as independent consultants. It combines what I've done, what I've experienced, and what works with the stories of real people. These are my personal reflections and conclusions, grounded in my own real work with real people in real organizations. I hope that sharing them will help others create careers that serve them well, whether that's inside an organization or owning their own practice.

CHAPTER 1

10 TRENDS PROPELLING
PROFESSIONALS TO INDEPENDENCE

It was a really good place to have a career, until one day it wasn't. Thirteen years earlier, RR Donnelley, a Fortune 200 printing company, had taken a chance on me. They had hired me as I was making a BIG career shift from nonprofit to for-profit, education to manufacturing, and working with children to working with adults.

It was a good run while it lasted. I loved the company and was proud of the work we did. After all, what was not to like about printing books? I had gotten my MBA and received a wide array of other professional development opportunities thanks to their investment in me. I had moved into a corporate role in middle management and had a wonderful boss and a great team. More importantly, I was doing work that made my heart sing.

And then came a merger, along with a new top leadership team and the inevitable reorganization and staff rationalization. My boss was given notice. My team was dispersed. And it was painfully clear that the work I was doing as an internal consultant and trainer on organizational change was not going to be what I did any longer.

I began to cry every day on my way into work. I was overcome with grief and sorrow for those who were losing their jobs. I was also gripped with personal grief for myself and the work that I loved, as I saw it slipping out of my grasp.

To this day, I'm not sure if it was an act of desperation or divine inspiration that made me decide to opt in to an offer of six months' severance. I was a planner, and I didn't have a plan. My income was central to my family's well-being, and I was giving up a well-paying job. I didn't have any idea how to do independent consulting; in fact, I only knew one other person who was doing anything remotely like this.

Nonetheless, with the support of my husband and an abundance of uninformed optimism, I accepted my severance package, rolled over my 401K, and determined that I had exactly six months (the duration of my severance payments) to figure this out.

There were concerned peers and friends who looked askance at my decision. They expressed doubt that anyone would pay me to do the work I so desperately wanted to do. They implored me not to give up the security of the known—a regular paycheck with a good company—for the risk of going it alone. I am eternally grateful that I didn't let the naysayers be my undoing.

And so, fifteen years later, I look back at that wonderful convergence of optimism and naivete, of courage and cluelessness, and offer extreme gratitude. That step of faith was followed by hard but joyful work. I have created a career for myself that enables me to do the work I love with clients I respect. I have far more earning power than I ever would have had in a corporate setting. And to top it all off, I control my career, rather than my career controlling me.

As I write this, I am sitting on the deck of our beautiful coastal home in North Carolina, overlooking the water. I have five weeks of vacation scheduled for this year, and I've been able to block out three entire weeks for writing. I am partnering with clients in work that really matters. I have several teams of amazing professionals working on those engagements with me. I am blessed by this work and the choice I made back in 2004.

And so, in this book, I want to share with skilled professionals that being an independent may be a choice for them. I'll share why it is easier and easier to do this, what it takes, and paint the path to get started. I'll be candid about the pitfalls, the problems, and the pains. And I will be crystal clear that this path is not for everyone.

What I am most excited about is sharing with you that you have a choice. You have a choice to find joy working with a good company—that was a great choice for me for many years. You also have a choice to step into an independent professional practice—that has been a positive, life-changing option for me. Either way, I encourage you to "own it," to take control of your career and to shape it in ways that serve you and the gifts you have to bring into this world in the best possible way.

It's More than Doctors and Lawyers

In a not so distant past, those of us who had professional skills got our degrees and then got our jobs. There were exceptions. Some doctors, lawyers, and an occasional CPA might open their own practice. For the rest of us, the choice was fairly black and white: work for someone else or don't work at all.

That has changed and continues to change rapidly. Another choice has emerged—the opportunity to be independent.

If you are an engineer, a manager, an IT professional, an accountant, a supply chain expert, or an HR professional—you have this choice. If you are a researcher, a scientist, a teacher, or a professor—you, too, have this choice. If you are a nurse, a doctor, or another health care professional—this is about you too. In other words, if you are a person who has skills you acquired post-high school and you apply those skills in a professional

> In other words, if you are a person who has skills you acquired post-high school and you apply those skills in a professional occupation, this opportunity is about you, and you are in the right place.

occupation, this opportunity is about you, and you are in the right place.

You may recognize the big shifts that are happening in the world of professional work. And you may know that times of disruption also are times of opportunity. But maybe you just have not been able to make sense of it all. That is exactly what we will do over the course of this book.

We'll begin by looking at the trends that are impacting professional work today and how they are supporting this second choice of professional independence. I'll share with you what independent consulting looks like and the traits successful independents share. I'll also be quite candid about the things that trip people up, and the warning signs that this is not a good career choice for you. I'll share with you things I didn't know before I started and sure wish I had. And throughout the book, I'll pose questions for you to consider if you are contemplating going independent.

This Fairy Tale is False

Your parents or teachers or professors most likely told you this fairy tale: Go to school. Study hard. Get good grades. That, little one, will set you up for a good job with a good company. You'll have steady employment, a good income, and a nice life. Of course, you will have to work hard. But that is the price you pay for all that security. Someday you'll reap the benefits of all that hard work. You'll retire. You'll finally have the time to travel. To enjoy life. And to live happily ever after. The end.

In fact, you may be telling yourself the same fairy tale. Or you may not only be telling yourself but also working hard to make it come true. Or you may be passing along that fairy tale to your children, your students, your nieces or nephews, or anyone under the age of 20 who will listen to you. Please stop doing that!

Your parents, teachers, and professors were not trying to deceive you. They truly wanted you to be happy and healthy and prosperous. But what they either didn't know or did not want to acknowledge is that the fairy tale world of professionals—stable jobs with great pay, amazing benefits, and steady work for decades on end—is dead. Gone. Period.

In its place is something different. More dynamic. More fluid. Constantly changing. Filled with challenges and perils. And yes, of course, with opportunities.

It is time to create a new narrative. A story that is less wishful thinking and more practical. One that works for professionals and organizations. One that enables you to be happy and healthy and prosperous. Not in the same way as the past, but in a new way. Let's learn more about what that new way might be.

Things are Different for Professionals Today

The landscape for professionals today is clearly different than it was in the past. Yet that statement has been true for each and every decade. The stability of the 60s gave way to the excesses of the 70s. The 80s were marked with the influx of women in professional roles, and the 90s saw America reestablishing itself as an efficient producer of quality goods. Then there was the digitization and automation that marked the millennium. Which brings us to today.

Independence as the New Normal

One very big change is that as a professional, you are highly likely, at some point in your career span, to work for yourself. And conversely, if you are leading others in an organization, you are likely to tap into this growing independent professional talent pool as an intentional strategy to do the work you are charged to do.

There are three primary forces that are fueling the disruption we face in professional occupations; each one amplifying the other two.

It is time to create a new narrative. A story that is less wishful thinking and more practical. One that works for professionals and organizations. One that enables you to be happy and healthy and prosperous. Not in the same way as the past, but in a new way.

One very big change is that as a professional, you are highly likely, at some point in your career span, to work for yourself. And conversely, if you are leading others in an organization, you are likely to tap into this growing independent professional talent pool as an intentional strategy to do the work you are charged to do.

Force 1: Technology

Without a doubt, technology is both a great disrupter and a great equalizer. This has both improved and deteriorated our quality of life. Technology has given humans the ability to compute, store data, and transmit data to foster exponential growth—and the end is not in sight. Connecting people via the web accelerates technology uptake, the pace of new knowledge generation, and the pervasiveness of technology in our lives. The internet of things means even the most mundane or obscure things are now "smart." In fact, a friend has a "smart" toilet.

This means that every profession, no matter your sector or your expertise, has become driven by technology. Professionals use technology to communicate, to analyze, to connect, to learn, and to manage just about all aspects of their jobs.

Technology clearly has shaped and will continue to shape not only what we do, but how we do it. Virtual work abounds. You can be part of a global team from just about anywhere. And that has provided a big boost to independents everywhere.

Force 2: Globalization: Professional Talent Anywhere, Anytime

Technology has enabled the shrinking of the world. Aided by the sophistication of our technology networks, I can easily communicate and collaborate with others, just about anywhere in the world. All I need is a reliable internet connection and a smartphone.

Another factor in the globalization of professional work is the increasing numbers of highly educated people in Asia and India. These countries, with already huge and fast-growing populations, value educational achievement in ways that have been lost in the USA.

Most of the work that has been the providence of the white-collar workforce in the US is now up for grabs. If I need to write code, I can scatter the talent coding across the globe, capitalizing on less expensive, highly motivated labor, and the ability to work around the clock without anyone having to work a graveyard shift.

Force 3: Acceleration of Knowledge Creation

Fueled by technology and fanned by the effect of connecting scientists and researchers and writers and thought leaders via the internet, the amount of information—both available to us and being created—is exploding. Each of us has more information at our fingertips in easily searchable formats than at any time in human history.

Consider these facts:

- Between 2016 and 2018, 90% of the world's data was created (Marr 2018)
- As of March 2019, 56% of the world's total population was connected to the web, and that percentage continues to climb quickly (Marr 2018)
- Thanks in part to the internet, television, and smartphones, we receive five times the amount of information that we did in 1986 (Alleyne 2011)

The triple impact of technology, globalization, and acceleration of knowledge directly impacts organizations and the professionals who work within them. The degree of disruption and pace of change is highly unlikely to either slow or decrease. Exactly how these three forces will impact your specific organization, your profession, or your job may be difficult to predict. Yet it is easy to predict that they will.

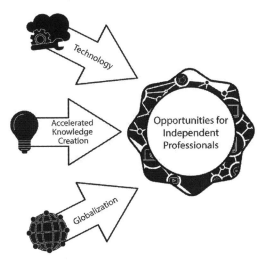

Top 10 Trends Impacting Independent Professionals

Any one of these three forces: technology, globalization, or the rapid increase in knowledge creation would pose challenges for our careers. Any one alone would be daunting. Together, they create an amplification effect, creating uncertainty on all sides. They interact with each other, creating unpredictable patterns, intersections, and effects.

The following ten are the trends that I see impacting our world of professional work today and in the next decade. They are in no particular order. But notice as you read through them, how interdependent they are. One affects the others. Also notice how, together, they create the impetuous for the career option of being an independent professional.

1. Sheer Numbers: Independents Outnumber Employees

As a professional, you are highly likely to work independently at some time, if not all, of your career. What was considered a stopgap way to earn some extra income between jobs is turning out to be a viable, long-term career option for many.

The shift in the workplace from employee to self-employed is fueled by ongoing job insecurity in traditional employment, enabled by technology, and accelerated by the increasingly demanding and unsatisfying work available for many professionals. More and more, talented professionals are opting out of full-time employment and choosing instead to go out on their own.

In prior eras, independents were either those quirky types who wanted to chart their own course or those "between jobs." Today, the trend is that the most talented and educated are opting to go independent, many of them immediately following graduation.

This trend was noted in a *Harvard Business Review* article called "The Rise of the Supertemps" (Miller 2012). The authors documented how the best and brightest graduates from prestigious schools (think Harvard MBAs) were opting to work independently rather than joining the organizations that were recruiting on campus. They asserted that this would be a growing trend way back in 2012.

The data proves them right. Current trends show companies using more and more highly skilled temporaries. Additionally, many highly skilled and experienced professionals are rejecting permanent jobs where demands are high, advancement is limited, compensation is capricious, and hours can be both long and inflexible.

In a 2018 report, Edleman Intelligence reports that the number of freelancers is growing faster than traditional employment and is poised to become the majority by 2027. More than 1 in 3 Americans freelanced in 2018, and the growth in freelancing is seven percent over five years, compared to two percent in traditional employment. And even more interesting: 51 percent of freelancers say that no amount of money would entice them to take a traditional job (Freelancing in America 2018). For an interesting infographic, go to /bit.ly/freelance2018.

If you are an executive needing top talent, don't be fooled into thinking these numbers are mostly college kids coding in their dorm rooms. This growing, independent workforce is likely to include the professional talent you need to compete. And if you are a professional, prepare for the fact that your best career option could be independence.

2. Technology Threats to Knowledge Workers

Just how artificial intelligence (AI), automation, and robotics will impact the work of highly trained and skilled professionals is uncertain. What is certain is that it will.

Pew Research reports that by 2024, technology will outperform human translators and that by 2049, AI will be able to produce a best-selling book. Professional jobs that require routine processes and algorithms (even though complex) are at risk of being done by a bot and not a human (Rainie 2017).

If you are a comp and benefits manager, bookkeeper, proofreader, market research analyst, or computer support professional, you should be worried in the near term (Bernassani 2017). And each of us, in some way, is highly likely to have AI do more tasks for us, even if our core function remains the same. In reality, every time we google something, ask Alexa, use GPS, spell check, or use auto-responders, AI is assisting us with our work.

Which raises the question—what jobs are less likely to be done by a machine and more likely to be done by a human? The answer is those that are complex in unpredictable ways, including those that require emotional intelligence (Rainie 2017). After all, what is more unpredictable than human beings? Jobs that require curiosity and creativity are also less likely to be done by a bot. While AI might reproduce or even compose a hit tune, playing jazz is a whole different level. Also, on the "safer list" are professions that require adaptability, resilience, and critical thinking. As such, I think this keeps the job of parenting safe!

The bottom line is this: AI, automation, and robotics are here to stay and will increasingly make inroads into work traditionally done by skilled and educated professionals. It will change the way we do our work and, in many occupations, will replace the work we have traditionally done.

3. Plug and Play: Modular Work vs. Traditional Jobs

As you step back and observe the pace of change in the world, it is hardly surprising that employers are no longer able to offer the type of job security they did in the industrial era. In fact, the top jobs of the future are not even "jobs" today. They haven't been created yet.

Change is too fast; skills become obsolete too quickly; and competition is fierce. Instead, new ways of assembling the necessary talent are emerging. These innovative strategies are nimbler, less durable, and better able to be reconfigured quickly and easily.

In some organizations, employee skills are in a shared data bank across the organization. Managers of projects and ad-hoc work can review the data bank and pull together the right team with the requisite skills in a matter of days—without cumbersome job transfers. These teams are formed and reformed as needs change, with employees acting more as "independent agents" than employees in a fixed job description.

Supplementing more fluid movement of talent inside organizations is the increasing use of outside talent on a short-term basis. McKinsey research found (in 2011) that 58 percent of US companies expect to use temporary arrangements at all levels (Manyika et al. 2011).

No matter what form it takes or how talent is tapped, work inside organizations is reflecting the external environment's demands for agility and speed. That means that work will be more transient; short-term projects will overtake jobs that last decades; and work will be done with a mix of employees, independents, and outside organizations.

> No matter what form it takes or how talent is tapped, work inside organizations is reflecting the external environment's demands for agility and speed. That means that work will be more transient; short-term projects will overtake jobs that last decades; and work will be done with a mix of employees, independents, and outside organizations.

4. Shorter Career Cycles Become the Norm

American society today tends to be organized around an industrial era view of life and career that looks very much like the fairy tale we encouraged you to debunk earlier in this book.

The old model was to spend the first two decades of your life learning, the majority of your adulthood earning, and then, if you were lucky, having the time, health, and wealth to enjoy the fruits of all your hard work. These large blocks of activity were focused on one thing and one thing at a time.

LEARN
Ages 5 to 25

EARN
Ages 20 to 65

ENJOY
Ages 60+

In today's environment, skills and careers become obsolete so quickly that you are highly unlikely to gain an education that will carry you through 20 years, let alone 30 or 40. In our current environment, you might have an employer for a decade but very seldom for life.

In today's environment, skills and careers become obsolete so quickly that you are highly unlikely to gain an education that will carry you through 20 years, let alone 30 or 40. In our current environment, you might have an employer for a decade but very seldom for life.

The new model that is emerging is one that has periods of learning followed by gainful employment, followed by some time to recharge or focus on your family, followed by learning new skills and using them for gainful employment. Repeat. Repeat. Repeat. And given that many have predicted that professionals today may have up to six different careers (yes—careers not jobs), the cycles may be even shorter than illustrated below.

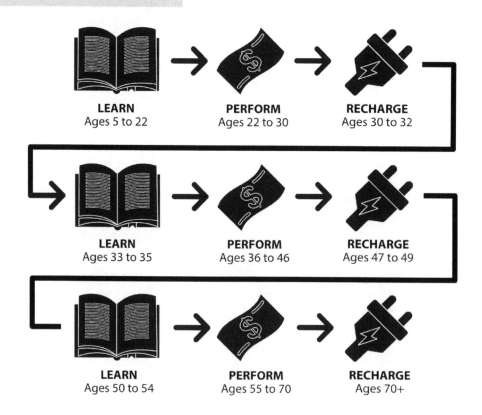

LEARN
Ages 5 to 22

PERFORM
Ages 22 to 30

RECHARGE
Ages 30 to 32

LEARN
Ages 33 to 35

PERFORM
Ages 36 to 46

RECHARGE
Ages 47 to 49

LEARN
Ages 50 to 54

PERFORM
Ages 55 to 70

RECHARGE
Ages 70+

Long-term planning for this new model will be virtually impossible. Careers in the future (like space pilot or nurse, space tourism guide, pharmaceutical artisan, fetus healer, or custom body part manufacturer) are unknown today but quite likely may be a hot job in the next decade (Paynter 2010). Even with functions that remain, such as accounting or engineering or sales or marketing, how that work gets done is likely to be dramatically different. Just ask anyone in marketing if their job is different today than it was ten years ago!

5. Demise of Desk Time

Technology has dramatically changed the landscape of how and where we do our work. In the past, workers were gathered together physically with a hovering leader close by. We were tethered to our technology, which was hardwired to the wall. And although, as professionals, we might not have punched an actual time clock, the watchful eye of our supervisors (and often our peers) monitored the time we arrived, the time we left, and the amount of time we spent at lunch.

We are now untethered. High-speed internet is available at the local coffee shop and in our homes. We have multiple high-powered devices which are portable, affordable, and enable us to conference call with someone in our car as we speed along the interstate. We can connect face-to-face (albeit virtually) with people in Tampa and Timbuktu.

This enables work to be done anytime and anywhere, which means that as a leader, your workers may not be right under your nose all the time. This means you will need to learn to manage a transitory, not always physically present work team. It also means that rather than time in the seat (our old measure of employee worth), as a leader, you will need to manage by total output and the quality of that output. In his book *DRiVE*, Daniel Pink cites a growing trend of firms moving to ROWE, or a Results Only Work Environment (Pink 2009). These environments have both high autonomy and high accountability—providing knowledgeable workers the opportunity to shape their work life in ways they want while delivering the agreed upon results.

This shift to being able to do most work from any location means that, as independent practitioners, we can serve clients across the globe wherever we are. Being a road warrior, once the hallmark of professional consulting, is no longer the way much independent work gets done. I, like many other independent professionals, can do my work anytime and anyplace, as long as I have my phone, PC, and a stable internet connection. I describe my work as location "agnostic."

6. Diverse by Design

The homogeneity of the workforce of the industrial era is gone, replaced by organizations filled with four (and sometimes five) generations—more women than ever before, more people of color, and an increasingly visible LGBT presence (they were always there, they were just afraid to let it be known). Technology enables people at all levels of the organization to work across geographies, introducing even more diversity in nationality, locations, and time zones.

Get stuck in the past on this one at your own peril. The most vibrant and creative organizations don't merely tolerate differences; they embrace them. A recent *Forbes* article cites a 2018 Boston Consulting Group study of 1,700 different companies across eight countries that had diverse management teams who were both more innovative and also had 19 percent higher revenue (Powers 2018). The link between diversity, creativity, and innovation is clear.

People that all think alike produce more of the same. If you add, embrace, and enable diverse thinking and experiences, creativity is sparked, innovation is fostered, and your understanding of diverse consumer groups is enhanced.

Creating organizations that are diverse by design is not altruistic. Leaders who embrace diversity are clear-thinking, smart business people. They know that the best

> Creating organizations that are diverse by design is not altruistic. Leaders who embrace diversity are clear-thinking, smart business people. They know that the best talent today comes in more than one hue, more than one gender, more than one "outer wrapper." And they know that to be successful requires creativity. And that creativity requires diversity.

talent today comes in more than one hue, more than one gender, more than one "outer wrapper." And they know that to be successful requires creativity. And that creativity requires diversity.

The desire to add diversity and to bring outside ideas in is a strong business case for hiring independent professionals. Independents can offer new perspectives, fresh ideas, and cutting edge skills, which is a compelling factor in the value proposition for using independents. It also means that the top consulting roles are no longer reserved for white males.

7. Agility Is as Important as Technical Skills

Industrial era organizations were all about reducing risk and driving efficiency through standardization. Size provided a shield from competitors and provided bargaining power with suppliers. This striving for stability was reflected in careers where professionals were hired for specific skills that were certified by degree and pedigree. Career paths were defined one move at a time. Things moved slowly. Opportunities came after you had paid your dues and showed you could perform, often taking decades.

While employers today are still hiring for specific skill sets, they are increasingly hiring for resilience, flexibility, and the ability to learn and adapt to new situations quickly.

> While employers today are still hiring for specific skill sets, they are increasingly hiring for resilience, flexibility, and the ability to learn and adapt to new situations quickly.

Given what we noted earlier about increasingly shorter career cycles, it is not difficult to see that both the drive and the ability to learn and learn quickly in challenging and ambiguous situations is a critical skill set. Just being smart in your area of expertise is not good enough anymore. The question becomes: how quickly and easily can you learn and produce in another area, and then another and then another again?

This is a critical trend to attend to, whether you are a student, an employee, or an independent. Learning agility is a skill—one that can be learned and honed. I believe that being successful as an independent is highly dependent on this skill. As such, you'll hear more about that later in this book.

8. Creativity and Innovation Are Coveted Skills

No matter your industry, consumer-facing business or B to B, innovation is an imperative, not a luxury. R&D is becoming central to a company's viability. Innovation is nurtured at all levels and expected of all employees. Organizational structures and processes are changing dramatically to innovate continually, test multiple ideas simultaneously, engage with customers and the market more directly, and to go to market with MVP versions (minimum viable product).

Organizations are adapting entrepreneurial methods (think Lean Start Up). They are redesigning how they are structured, how they do their work, and how they go to market in order to innovate, test, and then operationalize the best new products or services every day, all day long. And they are on the search for professionals who can help them innovate quickly; some will be employees, some will be fixed duration employees, and many will be independents.

9. Purpose Matters (More Than Ever)

I hate to tell you, but contrary to popular thought, profit is not the purpose of organizations. Nor is earning the most money you possibly can at the expense of everything else that has purpose in your life. Money is an outcome of successfully working toward a meaningful purpose. And you will find that finding the work that speaks to your purpose is much more rewarding than amassing even more "stuff." Which is not to say that money is evil; it is merely a means to an end.

In rapidly changing situations, a common phrase used is "I just want to get my feet on the ground." For good reason, for when things feel as if they are spinning uncontrollably, we seek something to provide grounding and focus. The one thing that can provide the grounding to guide our actions and enable us to stay afloat and pointed in the right direction during turbulent times is a purpose.

With a clearly defined purpose at the core, all else becomes a way to serve that purpose. External circumstances may change, and change quickly, but purpose is everlasting. And as you are buffeted by those changes, what you do and how you do it readjusts based on how you need to adapt your work to your purpose. Guiding to the North Star is an apt metaphor for this concept. Waves or wind might take your boat off course, but you can continually readjust if you keep the North Star is your guide. The more turbulent the environment, the more necessary having a core purpose becomes.

Purpose taps into passion. Purpose provides focus and agility. It builds consumer loyalty and employee engagement. It clears the clutter of disjointed KPIs and "flavor of the month" corporate initiatives.

The happiest and successful independent professionals I know have a purpose at their core. Every day they are living into what they feel is deeply personal and important for them. They strive to use their unique talents and signature strengths in service of that purpose.

We've all met professionals who have had big bank accounts and a bankrupt life. Their focus on work and financial wealth has compromised their physical health, their enjoyment of life, their ability to be a part of a community, and their accessibility for deep and meaningful family time. There are also independent professionals who lose sight of their purpose and get consumed by profit. But the funny thing is, I can't think of very many.

This career choice enables you to live into your purpose and to make a profit as an outcome. There is a synergistic phenomenon that I've seen happen over and over and over again. Do what you love, and you begin to bring abundance into your life. The abundance manifests itself in happiness and well-being and greater health. And very often, it also manifests itself in increasing financial wealth as well.

10. Nimble Networks Replace Bloated Bureaucracies

If one traces back the source of the industrial era's organizational structure of hierarchy and divisions and departments and chain of command, the path leads us straight to the military. Command to control. Rank, with its accompanying power. Top-down communication. Prohibitions of breaking rank or speaking truth to power.

These structures were designed in a time where stability was the key to success—where change, if necessary, was carefully introduced and then managed. Where plans were made in five- to ten-year increments, and "rocking the boat" was a bad thing. Where size was a competitive advantage and taking a decade to bring a new product to market was acceptable.

Today, speed matters. Decisions—and the information that fuels solid decisions—is dispersed across the organization. What is happening outside the organization is just as important, and one might argue even more important than what happens inside the organization. Technology provides us the platform to connect people, information, and ideas—and to do it quickly.

The new organizational structures that are emerging are more organic and less mechanistic. More flat than tall. More connected than controlled.

Organizational structures like these are more fluid, more nimble, and less structured to create space for bringing in temporary talent at all levels. As organizational boundaries become more porous, it is easier for independents to join project teams and to contribute fully. A newcomer with a needed skill set might have been seen as an outsider ten years ago, but today they are likely to be seen as an invaluable team member.

A Short Summary

The three forces of technology, globalization, and accelerated knowledge creation are dramatically changing careers for everyone. As a result, highly skilled professionals are seeing big shifts.

These three forces amplify each other and are resulting in these ten trends:

1. Sheer numbers: Independents Outnumber Employees

2. Technology Threatens Knowledge Workers

3. Plug and Play: Modular Work Replaces Traditional Jobs

4. Shorter Career Cycles Become the Norm

5. Demise of Desk Time

6. Diverse by Design

7. Agility is as Important as Technical Skills

8. Creativity and Innovation are Coveted Skills

9. Purpose Matters (more than ever)

10. Nimble Networks Replace Bloated Bureaucracies

Put those ten trends together, and it's easy to see how these forces are dramatically combining to reshape professional careers. It's easy to see why it is both possible and probable that you may be independent. And equally easy to see why companies are increasingly using independent professionals as a part of their overall talent strategy.

What Does This Mean for You?

I'll end every chapter with questions, not answers. This is done specificially for you as a professional who wants to own their career. And for good reason: Industrial era thinking was about certainty, clear direction, and directives. Twenty-first-century thinking is about ambiguity, exploration, and charting a way in unfamiliar places. Questions force us to think. They create possibility. They allow for creativity and enable us to craft an answer that works for us and our situation. And so, here are questions to consider from chapter one.

➡ As you review the Top Ten Trends, which ones are currently impacting you and your career?

➡ What are you doing to adapt to the trends that you are currently facing?

➡ What trends seem so scary that you are not even dealing with them?

➡ What steps are you taking to "own" your career?

CHAPTER 2
WHY PROFESSIONALS CHOOSE INDEPENDENCE

The Trend is Clear

The independent workforce is here, and here to stay. Fueled by uncertainty and rapidly changing skill requirements, hiring organizations look to highly skilled independents as a strategic option. Independents give them access to a skilled labor force without having to invest time in training their own and without the obligation of full-time employment.

Yet an equally compelling but unspoken fact is that full-time, long-term employment is becoming less and less attractive to many skilled professionals. Increasingly, jobs inside organizations are more and more prone to rightsizing, downsizing, and reorganizations. The security of working in a job with a "good company" is no longer a guarantee that your employment will be lasting.

Yet an equally compelling but unspoken fact is that full-time, long-term employment is becoming less and less attractive to many skilled professionals. Increasingly, jobs inside organizations are more and more prone to rightsizing, downsizing, and reorganizations. The security of working in a job with a "good company" is no longer a guarantee that your employment will be lasting.

For those employed in professional roles, the unrelenting pressure to produce combined with reduced staffing, tight budgets, and the expectation of being "on-call" 24/7 makes corporate jobs less luring. In the past, one might trade-off job security for a less-than-perfect fit or a highly stressful role. Now, with job security virtually nonexistent, the tradeoff feels less and less like a good deal for more and more professionals.

Today, the trend is shifting. Companies are using temporary labor across the entire organization by hiring outside professional consultants for highly specialized tasks. The new model aims to infuse both flexibility and talent into the workforce by tapping into the increasing number of qualified independent professionals across disciplines and skill levels. Sourcing these professionals is made easier by a host of midsize consultancies and boutique firms that provide talent across disciplines, such as IT, finance, marketing, HR, and sales.

There are other firms that find, vet, and subcontract contingent, professional labor. And increasingly, firms are looking to highly competent, locally available (or doing the work remotely), small independent consultants (a.k.a., freelancers) as a viable and cost-effective way to supplement their workforce.

Increasingly, talented, top-tier professionals are choosing independent consulting over traditional careers. A big reason is the freedom—more control over schedules and travel, as well as the freedom to say no to work they really don't want. It provides the opportunity to specialize in the work they most want to do and to become expert in. They can avoid the typical grunt work assignments that are necessary in organizations but unfulfilling. Independents find that income potential can be as good as or better than a traditional job, even with the cost of having to secure their own benefits and pay their own taxes. For many, escaping from corporate politics and the lack of control over their own job advancement is reason enough.

Top Six Reasons Professionals Choose Independence

In retrospect, my overt reason to go independent was to do work that was meaningful for me. And that was very true. Equally true was that deep down inside, I had a strong desire to create something of my own making.

I had a small taste of the intrinsic rewards of creating a business, back in the mid-1980s, when my dear friend Carmen Gatti and I were determined to overhaul the state of child care in our community—to improve the quality of care and the wages offered caregivers, to train staff well, and to engage parents in the process. In some ways, we were wildly successful—we launched six programs that accomplished all of the above in three years. But while we were successful programmatically, we failed at economic sustainability. The enduring lesson for me was the powerful intrinsic reward of creating something that both met a need and that I was passionate about. After three years of financial struggles, I chose to pack up, hand the business over to Carmen, and move to the Midwest. But inside me was a voice that said that I would start something else again, sometime.

As I reflect on my personal reasons and compare them to other professionals who have chosen to go it on their own, there are consistently six common reasons that compel really smart people to leave the security of a regular paycheck for the uncertainty of their own practice.

1. Control

In fifteen years of having my own independent practice, five years of teaching consulting at Purdue University, and two years of working with professionals who are launching their own independent consulting practices, there is one word that comes to the forefront to answer WHY I made this choice. And that word is CONTROL. Now, I know that control is merely an illusion—we truly have very little control over so much of our lives.

Let me provide some context. When we talk about having control, I believe we really mean choice:

- I can choose what skills I bring to the market and, consequently, the type of work I do.

- I can choose to work a little or a lot.

- I can choose how much I travel for work.

- I can choose how to structure my days and my hours.

- I can choose to take time off of work for reasons I don't have to share with others or get approval for or jeopardize my employment over.

- I can choose the type of clients I will work with.

- I can choose to fire a client.

In other words, I can put together my professional life in ways that work for me. And when circumstances in my life change, I can adjust accordingly.

Or as a peer of mine says, I make my own decisions, and the consequences are mine alone. I like calling the shots and knowing that even if I make a bad call, I can figure things out.

For example, when I first started my practice, I worked primarily on long-term engagements (six to eighteen months) that required me to be on the client site two to four days a week, and that required travel. It worked for many reasons. My children were grown. I only had to make two to three sales each year instead of thirty or forty. The work was steady and the paychecks reliable. I was able to deeply experience what life was like in a variety of industries and organizations, giving me more breadth and depth than I had from working with only one employer for fourteen years.

And that worked until it didn't. Eventually, the travel went from being exciting to being tolerable to being an energy drain. I felt I had lost a sense of community and was out of touch with friends and family. I was gaining new insights into my work of change and transformation but was locked into the old methodologies that I had built my practice on.

And so, as it often happens, the universe provided me a chance to reinvent myself. Two big projects ended within weeks of each other, and I didn't have the next engagement signed. My parents, who lived six hours away, needed more and more assistance. And seemingly out of the blue, I was offered a job teaching entrepreneurship at Purdue University.

I said yes to Purdue, which meant I had to say no to gigs that required extensive travel. I rebranded as Evergreen Leadership. I wrote a book. I found local clients. I used up all my Marriott points. I was home more nights than not. And all was good again.

I know that at some point, this too will no longer be the best fit for me. But I also know that when the next time comes for a pivot, I can exert that same level of control over my work and my working conditions, because I'm calling the shots.

The control that professionals yearn for is more of a say in how they work, what work they do, and when they do it. Far too many professionals feel they are at the mercy of organizations they work for. Their hours are stipulated. Their projects are assigned. The roles they are considered for are constrained by HR processes and policy. The expectations to be available all the time (nights/weekends/holidays/vacations) are immense. Job security is low, striking the fear that to push back, say no, or work less is like waving a flag that says fire me next.

> The control that professionals yearn for is more of a say in how they work, what work they do, and when they do it. Far too many professionals feel they are at the mercy of organizations they work for.

2. Flexibility

Flexibility, in some ways, is a variation on the theme of control. Control gives **you** the agency to make choices that affect your professional life, rather than your boss or some unknown policymaker at corporate. Flexibility means that there are many ways to do this work and that you can use your control to choose the ways to work that work for you.

Technology has supercharged the natural flexibility that comes with working independently. With technology, I can seamlessly flow between my Indiana and North Carolina offices on my own schedule. So much of my work is done either remotely or via teleconference, that I can be about anywhere in the world without losing productivity or client confidence.

In addition to location flexibility, independents have a great amount of flexibility about when they do their work. I'm a morning person, so I like to start at 7:00 a.m. and then take a break midafternoon. I might want to spend Monday doing something fun and then work on Saturday to do the work that needs to be done. While the times I am client-facing are nonnegotiable, the remainder of my work time is done when I want to do it. This does not mean the flexibility NOT to do the work—just when to do the work.

I've enjoyed the flexibility to scale up and then scale back down, based on personal priorities. There was a period of a few years when both my parents were near the end of their lives (increasing the demand on my time for hospital visits, doctor appointments, and escalated care), and my beautiful grandchildren were coming into our lives. I was able to scale back client engagements, allowing me to trek back to West Virginia for long weekends with my parents, help with late-night feeding support for my daughter's newborn twins, and to spend glorious Mondays caring for my granddaughter.

3. Fewer Office Politics

While I don't think this is the top reason professionals choose independence, I do think it is an extremely lovely benefit. It is like the job you select because the pay and medical benefits are good, and then you find out that you also have access to an amazing employee gym. Unplanned for but a nice surprise.

It doesn't matter how little or big your office is—there are always politics. There are frictions and factions. There are projects you are assigned that you absolutely hate. You are invited and expected to sit through endless and mind-numbing meetings.

As an independent, you can't completely escape the politics and the grunt work and the miserable meetings. You just have a whole lot less of it to contend with. For one thing, if you are charging $200 per hour, any budget-minded manager is going to be thoughtful about what meetings they invite you to and which ones they will just send you the actions item from, thank you very much.

In addition to fewer miserable meetings, there is a mindset shift that makes the office politics much easier to deal with. As an employee, it is so very easy to get sucked into the vortex of organizational dysfunction. You worry. You fret. You speculate (a fancy word for gossip). Even in your most objective moments, you know that power shifts happen, and there are those who are on the inside and those who are on the outside. And given that you've devoted a fair amount of your professional career to this joint, you want to land on the right side of the most recent power struggle. Your job, your advancement, and your career may depend on it.

As a consultant, you are most likely there to help with some of that dysfunction. And even if you aren't, you've been asked to affect some type of change, which almost always creates dysfunction of its own. Yet your role is to be above it, to be aware, to navigate around and through it, and at all costs, to avoid getting sucked into the vortex. Because you've not invested your entire career in this place with their particular problems, you bring a degree of perspective and objectivity that is helpful for your own mental health and the overall health of the organization you are working with.

> As a consultant, you are most likely there to help with some of that dysfunction. And even if you aren't, you've been asked to affect some type of change, which almost always creates dysfunction of its own. Yet your role is to be above it, to be aware, to navigate around and through it, and at all costs, to avoid getting sucked into the vortex.

That is not to say that you don't care. You do. That's not to say that you don't have to deal with it. You do. But your role is more like the emergency room triage professional who calmly assesses the situation, determines the best course of action, does what's necessary, washes your hands at the end of the shift, and walks away knowing you did what you needed to do.

4. Ability to Make More Money

As I left RR Donnelley, I joked with my-soon-to-be ex-coworkers that my goal was to work half as much and make just as much money. On paper that sounded possible. Over time, I've had some keener insights about the correlation between income, time, and effort.

First of all, getting started may require that you work twice as much and make hardly anything. I was diligent about tracking time and income in my first few years (due, in part, to the fact that I was billing by the hour). To my dismay, there were a few months in that first year where I worked a lot of hours, but very few that were billable. In fact, I clearly recall the month where I did the math and made the equivalent of $9 per hour. And that was before taxes and expenses. Lesson One: Your business is a startup, and not all startups make money at the beginning.

Once I began to get steady work, finances took a turn for the better. I was billing at $125 an hour (or $82.50 for work where I was a subcontractor). It was then that I learned Lesson Two: Not all of that money was mine to blow. Uncle Sam wants a chunk of that money, typically about 15 percent. And any business has expenses—independent consulting is no exception. Overhead can be kept to a minimum, but I still needed a phone, a PC, software, an internet connection, and a reliable car.

As I got busier, these types of financial insights continued to clobber me. Perhaps the most sobering realization was that my simple financial calculation of $125 per hours times 40 hours per week times four weeks per month (which adds up to a tidy sum) was not the way this work rolled. There was only one month that I billed more than 150 hours, and it just about killed me.

Lesson Three: Good months, for me, are when I can bill ten days a month. Not all months are good months. And billing ten days a month is not equivalent to only working ten days a month (remember that you have all those other things you need to do to run a business).

Lesson Four, though, is where the good news kicks in. As I became more established, I got more experience and was able to do higher-level work. I very intentionally invested in courses and certifications that continued to translate into increasing my market price or hourly rate. Over time, I've been able to give myself raises and not the measly one to three percent that was the norm in my corporate role.

My initial prediction was not quite true. I actually work more (although, most often, it does not feel like work) and earn a lot more than if I had stayed. And I'm having a lot more fun doing it!

5. Choose the Work They Do

I think most professionals have work that they are both good at and passionate about—the work that they feel called to do, the work that fills them up, the work that they can do all day long, and time flies.

For me, that is helping others improve their skills and performance through a combination of teaching, coaching, facilitation, and program design. As a corporate employee, the amount of time I spent in my "sweet spot" varied. In some roles, I did a fair amount, and in other roles hardly any.

As an independent professional, I can focus almost entirely on doing the work that I both do the best and enjoy the most. Of course, I have to do other things that I don't like as much, like accounting or upgrading my technology or responding to emails. But even those tasks are in service of allowing me to bring my skills and talents to those whom it will benefit.

Just as the market is going to put some limits on your fees, the market will also shape which of your talents and skills are able to get traction. I have a phenomenal community-based leadership development program that I love to do, and that gets amazing results. But, try as I might, I have been unable to find a sustainable market for this program. You may love coding in some obscure language, but unless there is a market for your work, you have a hobby and not a business.

I call this the power play. It is the intersection between what the market will pay for, what you have the skills to do, and the place where you find your passion. The power play is the Holy Grail. We are all in search of – where our skills, passions, and the market are in alignment.

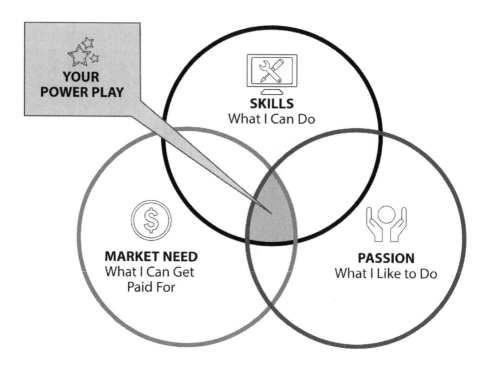

6. Choose Who They Work With

Another compelling perk cited by independents who have successfully done this work long enough to be established is the ability to choose whom they work with. In the beginning, you may feel your choices are not very broad. After all, when you don't have much work, can you really afford to be picky? Yet as you start to establish yourself as an independent professional, you begin to identify the clients that you work well with and the clients that you don't.

The criteria that independents use to decide who to work with can be as broad as a type of industry or as narrow as a particular role within a specific type of company. For example, I choose not to work with government contracts, as I find the paperwork required complex and the bidding system confusing. At the same time, I know several top-notch professionals who specialize in working with governments because they know how to navigate the system and enjoy working with large and diverse client groups.

Some independents will specialize in a particular industry, such as technology or utilities or consumer retail. Others define who they work with by company size or stage. I work well with larger companies, while others like to work with small startups or midsize privately owned firms.

My clients are sometimes surprised when I share that I am vetting them as much as they are vetting my firm and me. I lean more into psychographics than basic demographics, which means choosing to work with leaders who truly want to make a significant change in their leadership and organizations and are willing to partner closely with me over the course of the engagement. The moment I sense that a client wants to hand me this project and abandon the work, I find a way to decline the opportunity tactfully.

You Are Unique, So Are Your Reasons

Of these six reasons, I've found that the salience of each varies over time. When I first started, I was primarily motivated by doing the work I wanted to do and earning an income while doing it. After six years, flexibility became an important motivator. And in the last five years, the opportunity for me to use this work to give back has become a stronger and stronger reason.

Regardless of the primary motivations for going independent, it quickly becomes a way of life. In fact, my fellow independent peers have an inside joke that we are "unemployable" since this way of working works so well for us. I found it interesting that this 2017 Management Consulting Outlook says the same thing, just with more eloquent language and data.

A study conducted by Eden McCallum, *The Financial Times*, London Business School and INSEAD of 251 independent management consulting professionals in the EU and a group of their employed peers demonstrated that 91 percent are happy working as independent consultants. Notably, more than half who are happy said they are highly satisfied (53 percent). Several factors contributed to this – the most important being the intellectual challenge of the work. Another critical component was the differentiating factors between consulting for a firm and working as an independent – most notably, the ability to choose which type of work and the location of the engagement. It's worth noting that these independent consultants also report making more or similar money compared to when they were employed, with half indicating that they make more. It's also noteworthy that independent consultants see freelancing as a benefit for clients, as they believe the work provides more "bang for the buck," has a more significant impact and is more likely to be implemented compared to the work they did while at traditional firms. However, McCallum warns that freelancing isn't suitable for everyone. "Being an independent consultant is a fabulous choice for many, but for some, those without the relevant experience or without an entrepreneurial mindset, making the move could be a risky choice. Some will prefer life inside a big firm, with the financial security this brings. (GreenTarget 2017)

I concur. Independent consulting is not for everyone. I've seen plenty of really intelligent, hardworking, emotionally intelligent people plunge into going out on their own, and within less than a year, realize it is not for them. I meet regularly with people in transition from one employer to another who "consult" in between regular jobs yet are terribly eager to find their next company to work for.

The fact that consulting is good for some and not for others is not a condemnation. Those who do best while gainfully employed are no better or worse as professionals or people than those who can't ever even imagine being employed by a company on a full-time basis. It is like the difference between a cactus and a fern. Both are wonderful plants in their own right. But both have very different needs for climate, soil, water, and sunshine.

It is my hope that you make the right choice for you. If you explore this book and find that independent consulting is NOT for you, it will be time extremely well spent. If you explore this book and think independent consulting MIGHT be for you, it is a great beginning step. If you read this book and discover that independent consulting IS for you, it may give you the courage to begin.

But what really matters is your personal WHY. Getting clear on your reasons for considering independent consulting will help you decide if this is for you or if it is not. If you decide independence is for you, your reasons will shape the way your practice unfolds. There's no time like the present to wrestle with the questions below!

A Short Summary

Going independent is not for everyone. Those who do choose this career path typically do it for one or more of these reasons:

1. Control
2. Flexibility
3. Fewer Office Politics
4. Ability to Make More Money
5. Choose the Work they Do
6. Choose Who They Work With

What Does This Mean for You?

➜ Which of the six reasons described in this chapter resonates with you?

- Control

- Flexibility

- Income Potential

- Fewer Office Politics

- Choosing the Type of Work You Do

- Choosing Who You Work With

➜ What other personal reasons would you add?

➜ If you realized these outcomes, how would you feel about your career?

CHAPTER 3
WHAT DO INDEPENDENT PROFESSIONALS LOOK LIKE?

You may have a picture in mind of what a professional business consultant looks like. You might see them as working for a big, fancy firm. In your mind, they may wear a power suit and command attention. You suspect that they are a road warrior and someone who devotes themselves totally to work. You believe that they are educated, smart, and focused, but feel that you don't fit the profile.

On the other hand, if I asked what a small independent consultant looks like, you might be stumped. That may be because you don't know any (or you don't know that you know any). More likely, it is because they look like lots of different things. They are recent college grads and also professionals with decades of experience. They cut across gender, race, and geography. They might wear three-piece suits or sweats. They might have an office, work in a co-working space, or work from their home.

I'm going to introduce you to several professionals who are doing this. And I'll share, right now, the spoiler alert: There is no one formula, no one path, no one way to do this.

Ages vary. Education varies. The time it took to move from employee to independent varies. Yet there are some similarities. See if you can find them.

Katie McNamee

Founded Elevate Online immediately after college graduation in 2016. Cofounded LEAP in 2017.

Specializes in digital marketing with a focus on influencer marketing, content marketing, and web design.

I used to say Katie McNamee was "an exception." I stand corrected. Katie is truly exceptional but not an exception.

I first met Katie when she was a student in a consulting course I designed and taught in the Entrepreneurship Program at Purdue University. Every semester, 16 of our top students were selected from the program to take a capstone class, which paired teams of four students with local businesses to complete a consulting project.

For many, this course was their first exposure to the "real world" and to a place where there were real problems, actual consequences, and no ready answer in the back of the book. Invariably, semester after semester, there would be one standout team, mainly because that team had one standout student. And this particular semester, that student was Katie.

On the very last day of class, I asked the students to talk with me if they would be interested in doing a marketing internship with me that summer. I was thrilled to see Katie come forward. And she nailed it in the internship. Bright, strategic, hardworking, and insightful—and also able to work independently (key criteria in my practice, where all the back-office work is done virtually).

During this time, Katie was weighing her career options post-graduation. She clearly was marketable based on her field (public relations and strategic communication), her skill set (graphic design and strong social media marketing know-how), and her highly visible volunteer work with The Paint Crew (the student section for the Purdue men's basketball team). Yet as she interviewed for traditional jobs, she didn't find any that had both the work she wanted to do and were in a company where she wanted to work. Should she go to grad school? When she thought she had it all figured out with a major that was such a good fit, why was this transition to the world of work so challenging? In her words, "I thought I had it all figured out, and then it just didn't feel right."

Coming from a family of entrepreneurs, she kept circling back to striking out on her own. I made her a deal—for every 10 hours she worked for me, I would offer her one hour of coaching on starting her own business.

There came a crucial inflection point. We did a whiteboard exercise where we created a financial model. How much income did she need to make it on her own and move out of her parent's home? How much could she charge as a newly minted college grad? How many hours would she need to bill? How many clients would she need to get started? There was a click, with a resounding, "I can do this!" followed by, "I don't have a ton to lose. Now is the time."

The client from her capstone project became her very first paying client. She continued to work with me and then got another client and then another. Within a few short months, she moved into her own apartment as her business, Elevate Online, began to get a footing. As with most successful independent consultants, one engagement leads to another and another and another. As she approaches another year "on her own," she still believes that following her interests has not led her astray.

In the summer of 2017, I asked Katie to join me in a partnership role in LEAP, a new venture to support professionals who are launching and growing independent consulting practices. I said to her, to others, and to myself, that successful independent consultants looked like me, not like her. That you needed 20+ years in your field to be credible. That she benefited from her social media experience because many business owners believe that if you are under the age of 25, you are an expert. That Katie was an exception and that independent consulting or freelancing was not a viable career choice for most twenty-somethings. It turns out I was wrong—dead wrong.

In reality, the data tells a different story. A 2017 study by Edelman Intelligence reports that 50 percent of all freelancers are millennials (Lesonsky 2019). And over half of millennials are freelancers. In the current world, organizations are flat, job demands high, and job security a thing of the past. It makes the idea of working independently seem like a smart move—having a portfolio of multiple clients (most average 4 to 5) rather than one employer.

So yes, I was totally wrong. Katie is not an exception. Half of her peers are making exactly the same career decision—to go out on their own and go after freedom and flexibility rather than the professional, corporate job.

Alexandra Rufatto-Perry

Founder of Practically Speaking.

Offers professional speaking and communications coaching.

Alexandra Rufatto-Perry is on the cusp of realizing that she's onto something big. She is just barely getting past the persistent internal dialogue that asks her if she can do this big thing. And she is just starting to believe—to really believe—that yes, indeed, she can.

Her 17 years as a speech and language pathologist fostered keen learnings. She understands how the human brain works in relation to speech, language, and communication. She then practically and effectively applies that knowledge to help others improve their speech and communication skills.

Yet it was a stranger that sowed the tiny seed that has sprouted into Alex's consulting practice, Practically Speaking. She was speaking to a group in Plainfield, Indiana, and she shared some personal stories. No big stage. No important audience. But afterward, one woman came forward and asked Alex if she would work with her to improve her ability to communicate. Something was sparked.

She was astonished and then curious. Could she use what she knew about communication and people and the human brain to help others outside of a clinical setting? Could she help people communicate more clearly and more confidently? She started thinking, then journaling, and eventually brought the idea up with her husband, Clark, who was supportive. Finally, she invested all of five dollars on Fiverr for a business card. Not a great one—but a real business card, nonetheless.

For the first year, she hustled to build her business, while continuing to do part-time speech and language therapy work at a clinic. She wasn't sure if this was a business or a hobby. But she kept reaching out to people and learning how to step into this new career that promised control, flexibility, and the chance to do the work she loved with clients that she wanted to work with. In Alex's words, it was both fabulous and scary.

It took about 18 months after that first Fiverr business card for her to get traction. Now she has real paying clients. She has built a solid network and reputation. She just did her first Ted Talk and is getting national speaking gigs. She is on her way, one step at a time, to realizing her dream of success. A dream where her business is more than a hobby, and she has enough earning power to allow Clark, her husband, to pursue his dreams.

Rhett Campbell

Chose independence after 37 years of professional experience.

Offers services as outsourced VP of Sales as part of the Sales Xceleration Network

Rhett Campbell is a natural—a natural networker and entrepreneur, that is. It just took him almost four decades to find his stride. Rhett did what many of us were advised to do—go to college, find a good company, work for them for a long time, move up, then up some more, and then up some more. For 30 years, that worked, as Rhett moved up from his start as a territory sales rep through a series of promotions. And as Rhett toughed it out in his senior-level position during working years 31 to 37, he found something that surprised him. The more he moved up, the more resistance he got to his ideas, the less of a difference he was able to make—and the expectations were bigger.

It was a conversation with a neighbor that enabled Rhett to finally say goodbye to the title, the salary, and the "golden handcuffs" that chafed more and more with each passing year. That neighbor introduced him to Mark Thacker, founder and president of Sales Xceleration, a firm that equips people like Rhett to succeed as a consultant for companies who need help with sales.

It took three months of discernment and worrying about whether he could do it before Rhett retired after 37 years and began to "own it." There were doubts. There was concern about making it financially. And there was the hard reality that after 37 years, no one really missed him at his old company.

Rhett is now president of Vantage Selling Solutions. He is making a difference with the two to three clients he serves at a time. He is able to be himself, something he never felt comfortable doing in his corporate role. He has built an amazing network and a solid, successful business. And by the way, financially he is just fine. In his words, "When I stopped worrying about money and saw it instead as a by-product of doing good work for my clients, I made money. Now I enjoy every day, and I didn't always feel that way."

Alana Robinson

Cofounder of Robinson Consulting Group after 30+ Years industry experience.

Offers services as Interim CIO and Enterprise IT System Expert.

Those who meet Alana Robinson remember her. Perhaps it is her warm laugh (often at herself) or her wit or her will. Combined, she is a powerhouse of a woman who has powered through six companies, seven relocations, 14 distinct roles, and since 2004, numerous pivots as co-owner with her beloved husband, O'Neal, at Robinson Consulting Group, Inc.

I first met up with Alana as she led an enterprise-wide effort to modernize, standardize, and integrate the technology that ran the company we worked for, RR Donnelley. We both made the choice to leave that same company in 2004 and go independent. Now, over 15 years later, we agree on two things: our time in that company had been good, and establishing a consulting practice is even better.

Alana had dreamed about having a company of her own, but those dreams had no details. Her exit from RR Donnelley provided the window of opportunity to evaluate her options—to seek further employment or to establish a new track record as a successful entrepreneur.

And so, Robinson Consulting Group, Inc., was the answer. Past relationships (remember all those jobs and all those companies?)

began to call with opportunities. A two-year project in Boston. What started as a two-day gig was so successful that they asked her to come back for two months and then two years. Consulting helped Alana and O'Neal get through financial challenges following a failed franchise fiasco. It also led her directly to a career and life that (in her words) is rewarding, flexible, challenging, and creative. Her final descriptor: "A Blessing."

In Alana's words, this "Entrepreneur/Consulting" career choice requires a combination of self-confidence, openness to evolve, and willingness to take risks. And yet, don't think that once it was decided, it was done. In the fourteen years of founding, launching, and growing RGC, there were many "choices to change." There was the 2008 and 2009 recession when corporate enterprise IT work vanished. They weathered that by leveraging O'Neal's experience in higher education and finance. RGC consulted with nine universities over five years. And then another opportunity arose, and they shifted again—into the public sector. With each change, Alana became more confident that they could respond to changes effectively. Each shift became easier and more fluid.

When asked what the best part is of independent consulting, Alana summed it up this way: "This has positioned us to create a legacy for our grandchildren. Part of that is a financial legacy. More importantly, it is the legacy of being a role model, for them to know that they have options and that they, too, can pursue a passion to be a business owner."

Karl Riddett

Data and Analytics Expert.

Currently employed at Interworks and on a path to independence.

Karl Riddett graduated from Georgia Tech in June 2000 with big ambitions. He took a job with a large, fast-growing fast food chain. Over 13 years, he moved up the ranks in the IT department until he decided to become an "operator" or owner of a franchise. It was there that things began to fall apart. He got a DUI, which led to an ultimatum from his wife. If he didn't stop drinking, she was going to leave him. Combined, those events forced him to admit to his addiction to alcohol and acknowledge the need to make big changes in his life. Almost 20 years later, those big changes continue to provide him with a purpose and fuel his passion for helping others.

Karl has a vision, even though the exact details are yet to be worked out. It is a vision that combines his passion for helping others in the most crucial part of their recovery from addiction with his wife's passion for rescuing dogs. She has rescued over 2,000 dogs in the last 20 years. The couple has an average of 20 to 25 dogs in their home at one time, which may push the definition of passion into an obsession.

Someday in the future, Karl and his wife, Chandler, plan to open Recovery Ranch. It will be a safe place that will give recovering alcoholics a safe place to live between exiting a treatment facility and entering the world at large. They know this is especially critical for those without family or other support. Recovery Ranch will pair humans who need a place and a purpose with dogs that need a safe place and care. It is the perfect integration for this husband/wife duo.

There are a number of things that must come together for Karl and Chandler's vision to materialize, including money to invest while also sustaining their family of six. This will require a career that not only provides income but also provides flexibility. Karl is learning the ins and outs of consulting.

And so, post recovery, Karl joined another corporate organization and honed his IT and leadership skills. With expertise in business intelligence, data visualization, and dashboard creation, Karl then joined InterWorks. In this role, he splits his time between service delivery to clients and business development. He is gaining valuable experience learning how to work with clients and, even more importantly, how to sell consulting services.

By his own admission, Karl is not "chasing titles" anymore. Instead, he is chasing a purpose, a passion, and a vision. He traded lucrative corporate bonuses for rich learning, meaningful work, and building a pathway to Recovery Ranch. He's lost the three hours of daily commuting and gained more time with family, even with the overnight travel that is sometimes required in his new job.

Is it worth it? Talk to Karl, and you know it is. And you also know that this is a pathway for him to a deep and meaningful purpose. One which will be his ultimate measure of success—maximizing his talent (and not just his money and time) in the service of others. He's making a difference to those he interacts with daily and, ultimately, leaving a legacy.

Aaron Pritz

Founded Reveal Risk after 17 years of business experience at a Fortune 200 firm.

Specializes in cybersecurity, privacy, risk management, and fractional CISO.

Some would say walking away from a leadership role with a Big Pharma company was bold, especially after 17 years of increasing responsibilities and with more room to grow professionally. Others might say it was risky. Others might even say it was foolish. Yet to Aaron Pritz, the IT leader who left Eli Lilly in December of 2017, it was exactly the right move at exactly the right time. In his words: "I have no regrets. Every aspect of it is better."

This is not to say his time at Lilly was a dead end. In fact, nothing could be further from the truth. It was that time that beautifully equipped him to step out and form Aaron Pritz and Associates. Then, 18 months later, he cofounded Reveal Risk, a consulting firm specializing in cybersecurity and risk management.

In those 17 years with a big corporation, Aaron honed his skills in audit and risk management. He learned how to work with diverse teams across the globe. He became a six sigma black belt. He was a key leader in the cybersecurity organization—learning in the trenches how big the risks were and how to use a multi-faceted approach that leveraged technology and engaged with the workforce to minimize cyber threats. And now he offers his deep expertise to a variety of firms across industries.

Aaron was thoughtful about how he made the transition. He exited during a corporate downsizing event, which provided him severance pay. He subcontracted his first few engagements. Yet early on in his professional consulting career, it was clear to him that this indeed was the right choice at the right time.

April Petrey

Automotive industry implementation expert with 20 years' experience.

Current employee on the path to independent consulting career.

There is one thing that emerges over time—and that is the ability to see the patterns and contours of one's life. Such is the case with April Petrey.

She currently has what many would want in a career: interesting work, stability, and a good income. And yet, there is something vital missing—April doesn't feel challenged.

As a result, she has been on a quest to start her own consulting practice. And in typical April fashion, she is doing it with passion, persistence, and patience.

Her time working for others over the past 20 years has honed her skills in systems thinking, training, sales, and operations. She's built an extensive network of people who have experienced her ability to get results. And she has been quietly, but consistently, building her runway to launch an independent consulting practice.

Going out on her own was about the last thing April thought she would do. She had sometimes imagined opening her own business. But she had envisioned selling a product or service—certainly not selling herself. After working with a career coach and spending nine months seeking the "right" job (and finding there were none), it became clear that this was exactly what she needed to do. And so, April began her quest to create her own career on her own terms and at her own pace.

April has not left her employer yet, but she is working on her plan. She has set up her consulting company and has gotten certified as a coach. She has been diligent about building her bank account—slashing expenses and moving into a smaller, less expensive home.

She has also started to do some side gigs in the evenings and on weekends. April is not certain when the time will be right to leave her employer and be totally on her own. But when that time comes, she is certain that she will be ready.

A Short Summary

In this chapter, I've shared how seven different professionals took very different paths to "owning it." These are only a few of the stories I could tell about going it on your own. No one story is the same. No one path is identical.

There is no one way to move into independence. Some have been independent for a long time; others have yet to make the leap. Some started in their twenties, others in their sixties. What they do share is a marketable skill set, a passion for their work, and a desire to "own it."

What Does This Mean for You?

As you read through these stories of real people making real-life choices to own their careers, reflect on these questions:

➜   What story is most like your own?

➜   Which of these independent professionals inspired you? Why?

➜   Where are you on your own journey?

➜   What might be a great next step for you?

CHAPTER 4

HOW DID WE GET HERE?
A BRIEF (I PROMISE) HISTORY

The Fairy Tale Was True

Remember that fairy tale from chapter one? Go to school, study hard, get a good job, work for decades, move up the ladder, be successful, retire ... then, live happily ever after?

Believe me when I say it existed. Because it did—in America, at least. While it was mostly accessible to those who were educated, white, and male, it existed in the era following World War II. For a few fleeting decades, corporations grew to stabilize their profits, rather than to maximize them. Certain profits, the thinking went, were the result of long-term planning based on solid analysis and stable, well-trained, and ready employees.

Large, steady, and predictable defined both the business strategy and the employment picture. Lots of employees, committed to over the long haul, doing well-defined jobs with specific requirements, and a well-planned career path—a path that paid a living wage. The premise was that if you did what was asked, the corporation looked out for you.

Of course, the fairy tale didn't come true for everyone—especially if you were female or a person of color. But it did come true for many. And I was the recipient of that stability. My father worked for the power company for thirty-plus years, which allowed us to have a stay-at-home mom and enough income for housing, meals, and a few luxuries. My parents were joined by many in the post-WWII economy that started in the late forties and lasted through the sixties.

In some industries, that stability continued well into the seventies, eighties, and nineties. I joined one of the largest printers in the late 1980s, and they were just beginning to grapple with the fact that business as usual was not usual at all.

I've come to learn that the seeds for the insecurity that we currently face were actually planted way back in the early fifties, at a time when they were hardly noticed.

How Did We Get Here?

The first cracks in this world appeared slowly in the mid-50s and were almost indiscernible. One was the use of temps. Another was the advancement of technology. Each development, viewed alone, has resulted in significant changes. Together, they amplified and accelerated changes in the way we do our work.

Temporary Labor at the Top and Bottom

When Elmer Winter founded Manpower in 1948 in Milwaukee, he did so out of his own need to hire a secretary—not forever but just for a few days. He had the insight that others might have that exact same need and built on that simple idea to create the first temporary agency. Although it was called Manpower, it was women (typically married white women who needed to earn some supplemental income), who were the foundation upon which the company was built. In fact, by 2017, the company employed three million people (Hyman 2018).

At about the same time, companies were hiring a far different kind of temp employee. They were white men. They were highly paid and were asked to help shape the strategy and direction of the largest and most powerful firms. They were called consultants. McKinsey and Company, founded in 1926 with a focus on accounting, spawned a number of bigger consultancies that grew their influence far beyond accounting and into many other functions of large organizations: operations, strategy, project management, quality, HR, and audit. This, too, was temporary work, albeit at a much different level.

McKinsey and Manpower both got their foothold in the US market in the 1950s, and then both expanded their offices and methods globally in the 1960s. They had different business models and targeted different office demographics, but fostered common beliefs that ran counter to prevailing business wisdom:

- Temporary employees can replace permanent ones at all levels.

- Temps can be brought in when workloads are high, enabling firms to staff to the lowest demand rather than the highest.

- Temps can be hired for spot demands for particular skill needs.

- Temps are a way to try before you buy, putting talent through a long audition before actually hiring them into the regular workforce.

In the 1960s, size and stability as a business strategy took a perverse twist. Diversification was the mantra, and companies started growing by buying other companies, most often in industries or markets they knew nothing about. The idea was that bigger was better; diversification diminished risk; and smart MBA managers, guided by even smarter consultants, could reduce risk and maintain steady profits.

Enter in a few businessmen who found that they could create wealth on paper through trading, buying, and selling companies. Rather than create true value, they manipulated the market, creating conglomerates whose value on the books far overstated their actual value. The inevitable thing happened in the late 1960s—the bubble burst. And with it came increasing skepticism about corporations, especially big ones.

Then, in the 1970s, business thinkers like Warren Bennis and Peter Drucker began to sound the warning that organizations needed to be more fluid, more flexible, more organic—bureaucracy would be defunct (Hyman 2018). What they predicted way back then is now unfolding. We are now seeing:

- Employees who don't have jobs but move in and out of teams

- Executives as organizers of these teams

- Adaptive, rapidly changing temporary systems

- Quick, intense relationships between workers and employers, rather than long-term commitments by either party

- Employees becoming entrepreneurs

And then, in the 1980s, office automation began to accelerate, causing a cascade of jobs, both white and blue-collar, to be eliminated, streamlined, outsourced, or off-shored. Toward the end of the 1980s, temps were seen as a normal part of a well-planned labor force. By 1988, over 90 percent of businesses used temps in some capacity, as reported by Manpower (Hyman 2018).

The 1990s came—and with them, a recession. This recession brought a move toward lean—lean thinking, lean processes, and lean staff. Downsizing hit hard, and mid-level professionals lost their jobs and their security in unheard of numbers. This was the decade that the unspoken promise of a secure job for loyal service was visibly and viscerally broken. Layoffs were measured in the thousands and took on a new normalcy (Davis 1998).

This leads us to today, where we find the two trends in temps expanding to create room for independent professionals in that middle space.

Making Room in the Middle

It took Manpower and McKinsey to introduce the notion of using temporary talent, albeit at very different levels in the organization. Manpower temps typically came in at the bottom with quickly trainable, repeatable skills. What started as temporary office work (answering the phone, typing, filing) spread to the factory floor, and eventually, to any jobs that were repeatable, replaceable, and trainable in short order.

McKinsey temps (and others from the Big Four) came in at the top. Their work required unique and highly developed skills—for work perceived to be important enough that you wanted to bring in the best.

> It took Manpower and McKinsey to introduce the notion of using temporary talent, albeit at very different levels in the organization.

What we are now experiencing is the growth of using temporary talent in the middle—for highly skilled work across the organization or professional-level work in HR, finance, accounting, IT, operations, quality, supply chain, and marketing.

Many times, this work in the middle is done via an agency, be it Manpower or a host of other firms. Yet the ability to find and source talent directly has been made easier by technology. In years past, you went to an agency because it was the only way you knew how to access temporary talent. Today, you can do a Google search, check LinkedIn, or use any of the many online services to find and source top talent for your projects and problems. And as a freelancer, you can use any number of online services to connect you with the people that need your skills.

Technology at Your Fingertips

Another big thing that initially didn't seem like very much appeared in 1995—the first web browser, Mosaic. This led to the World Wide Web. Which quickly changed, forever, the way we work.

In 2018, a study by Zug, a Switzerland office provider, indicated that 70 percent of professionals globally work remotely at least once a week, and 53 percent work remotely for at least half the week. Technology is what enables this trend (Browne 2018).

Although it may sound romantic—working from home in your PJ's and tapping into the best talent from twenty different countries—there is a dark side as well. Just because it is easy to always be connected, that does not require us to be connected 24/7. But often we act as if it does. Working globally means compromises in work hours to meet across time zones—US-based individuals may end up working very early hours, while those in Europe might work very late, and those in Asia and Australia might end up working the equivalent of a graveyard shift.

Whether in response to rising real estate costs, the need to tap into talent, or the desire to attract younger talent (for whom working remotely is attractive), working remotely is here and here to stay. And with that comes the need to rethink how work is defined, allocated, and measured. New tools and technology are required, as well as leaders who can lead in dramatically different ways. And it clearly paves the way for an increasing number of skilled professionals to do their work anytime and anyplace.

This is a Very Brief History

This overview truly has been very brief. But in these few short pages, I've outlined two historical shifts that impact each and every professional and their careers:

1. Use of temporary talent as a strategic business tactic to control costs, manage fluctuating workloads, and source higher-level skills

2. Impact of the World Wide Web and increasingly powerful technology that enables work to be done virtually and in any place at any time

What Does the Future Hold?

I wish I had perfect future vision, but I don't. However, it does not take much of a leap to see that things are moving more quickly and with shorter timelines. Organizations have to figure out how to define, staff, and manage work faster than ever before. That ambiguity coupled with competitive market forces means that companies are doing what makes perfect sense—defining and managing work in smaller increments with shorter time horizons and with fixed duration assignments. And they are increasingly using independent professionals to get things done.

This means that formal organizational charts will move from fixed boxes to flexible networks of teams and work projects. It means that you may not be hired for a specific job, but instead for a particular skill set you bring that can be deployed across the organization and possibly changed throughout the year. More work will be done with mobile and modular teams, which are assembled and disassembled based on the timing of the work, rather than on a function or business unit.

> Employment for life becomes an anachronism. You view your career and career options as shorter assignments over the span of your working life. You may well spend some of your career inside an organization and some time on your own.

You might support several teams simultaneously, rather than just one. Very structured career and promotional paths will be replaced by flexible assignments and learning opportunities. In this new structure, you act as your own agent, managing and overseeing opportunities. Employment for life becomes an anachronism. You view your career and career options as shorter assignments over the span of your working life. You may well spend some of your career inside an organization and some time on your own.

Whether you are on the inside or on your own, you have an imperative to own your career. Your boss is not responsible for your career. HR is not responsible for your career. You are responsible for your career and your success. You must "own it."

> Prepare yourself for a career shift—either inside your organization or outside it. Because odds are, you'll not be in the same place doing the same thing for long.

My advice is this: During those times when you are employed, know your strengths and find ways to use them at work. Seize opportunities to grow and develop if they are offered. And if they are not, create them or seek them out on your own. Take some measured risks and get better and better at dealing with ambiguity. Prepare yourself for a career shift—either inside your organization or outside it. Because odds are, you'll not be in the same place doing the same thing for long.

A Short Summary

Temporary talent is here to stay. In the middle of the 20th century, Manpower introduced the concept of using a temporary workforce force with trainable, repeatable skills as did McKinsey, who offered highly skilled and highly compensated consultants. Using temporary labor is now widely accepted, with organizations seeking temporary talent at all levels of the organization.

What Does This Mean for You?

- How is the increasing use of temporary talent impacting my industry? My company?

- What have I done in the past year to increase my professional skills and value to the organizations I serve, either as an employee or an independent?

- What have I done in the past year to challenge myself to do something different?

- What is one thing I could do in the next 30 days to "own" my career?

CHAPTER 5

WAYS TO STRIKE OUT ON YOUR OWN

On April 1, 2004, I decided to leave the company I had worked at for thirteen plus years. It may have been serendipity, but that date also happened to be my 50th birthday. Within the week, I had signaled my intention to take severance to my new boss. Within two weeks, it was a done deal, with an exit date of May 31st.

By mid-May, I had my first opportunity for a professional engagement. Through a series of introductions in Chicagoland, I was connected with Marion Cook, who was the principle of Ageos Consulting. She needed someone with my skill set for a client in Wisconsin and asked if I was interested in subcontracting. Of course, I said yes. And then I panicked. I had no idea how to do this. Nonetheless, in short order, I had my first engagement and my first head dunking in the world of consulting. Luckily for me, Marion guided me that first time around.

Throughout my independent career, I've completed work through a variety of arrangements. I've subcontracted. I've freelanced and billed by the hour. I've collaborated with peers on joint ventures. I've done many fixed price, large engagements. I've been on retainer. But no matter what shape the work took on, I've been independent in the market with my own brand.

The point is, as an independent professional, you have a variety of choices in how to structure your work. Each approach has unique pros and cons. In this chapter, I'll walk you through some of the most common arrangements. A word of warning: this is not an "either-or" choice. Some independents will only utilize one method, while others will combine several of them. It is helpful to know the options as well as the pros and cons of each.

Freelancer

Professionals who freelance are what comes to mind when we talk about the "gig" economy. These workers might freelance either part- or full-time, working from home, or in a collaborative working space. Others freelance as a "side hustle." A few decades ago, we would have called it "moonlighting." Moonlighting happened when you were employed by one employer and took a job with a second (or third employer) after hours or on the weekend. Today, your side hustle likely means that you are doing work on your own and are hired job by job. For many, the side hustle serves as a proof of concept for a business launch, or to test if they could, indeed, make a go of it alone. As such, I find more and more professionals who have a side hustle during their off-work hours.

Freelancers are often called 1099 employees since instead of the W-2 tax form issued to regular employees, they are issued a 1099 to report earnings to the IRS. Corporate C Level folks might also call them "off balance sheet" labor, as their wages are accounted for differently than the obligations associated with regular W-2 employees.

Freelancers typically string together a series of small jobs with a variety of clients. They may be paid by the hour or for a specific task or deliverable. For example, you might hire a freelancer to build a website for you at $70 per hour. Or you might work with a freelancer to develop your site for a fixed fee, perhaps $4,500 if it is not too complex.

Several online services are available to match freelancers with those who want to hire them, including Upwork, Guru, Freelancer.com, Mechanical Turk (Amazon's entry into the online freelance marketplace), Toptal, Fiverr (where jobs are sold in increments of $5) and of course, Craigslist.

The variety of work done by freelancers is wide. IT work is big, as is marketing. But think broadly—from virtual assistants to virtual attorneys, almost any professional body of work that can be done using technology is an option for freelancing.

Professionals are attracted to freelancing for a variety of reasons. These include supplementing a regular income, the freedom to choose their own hours, having more control over the work they do and the people they work with, and working wherever they want to. Freelancers can also make more per hour than if they worked through an agency or subcontractor, who must cover their expenses for being in the middle. The markup might be as little as 15 percent or as much as 50 percent depending on the field, the firm, and the market rates.

Of course, with that freedom, comes responsibilities. Freelancers may get to keep the entire hourly rate, but that rate needs to cover the work/time required to find, secure, and manage clients. Part of managing clients means handling unhappy customers or projects that go south. It may mean tracking down payments and working hard to get clients to pay you—on time and, at times, just to pay you what you are owed.

A hard reality of freelancing is that the work and the pay can be erratic. Unlike a paycheck where a set amount that drops into your bank account like clockwork, freelancers have variable income—all the time. Sometimes it depends on the amount of work. Sometimes it depends on the timing of the work. And a lot of it depends on the reliability of client payments.

Perhaps the biggest challenge for freelancers is the lack of benefits. These include no health care, no retirement plans, no paid days off, or any of the other host of benefits those employed by an organization take for granted. Of course, these can all be planned for and bought on the open market, but that $75 per hour starts to shrink rapidly when you take out taxes, health care, and retirement savings.

Subcontract / Work with an Agency

Subcontracting, or working with an agency for placement, is a way that many professionals build flexibility and control into their work life, without the burden of business development and engagement management. Many specialty agencies place professionals—from accounting to IT to HR to sales and marketing. There are local firms, national firms, and international firms.

Increasingly, both the large and midsize consulting companies are using a mix of consultants for their engagements, blending full-time employees with 1099 staff. For example, Price Waterhouse Cooper blends the two with their PWC Talent Exchange, where they source independent professionals to supplement their project teams. Another innovative example is the firm Your Encore, which matches retirees in life sciences and consumer goods with companies that are looking for senior (in age and experience) talent. And many small to midsized firms look to trusted subcontractors to form teams needed for larger client engagements.

My consulting practice, Evergreen Leadership, is entirely built on subcontracted talent. Once I define an engagement with a client, I extend invitations to a trusted group of approximately 20 "Practice Partners." Each of the practice partners has their own independent consulting practice but is interested in working as a team on projects with me.

At times, I engage only one or two practice partners. At other times, I engage a team of six to eight. This model is a win-win-win—for our clients, for my firm, and for my practice partners. Clients get hand-selected, top-notch practitioners for a reasonable price point and I to manage the engagement and the team. My practice partners can focus on the work they like to do, without the task of finding, selling, or managing the work. Additionally, we all benefit from working as a part of a professional team, which fills a void that many independent professionals struggle with. Independence can be lonely. The benefit to my firm is that I have a vetted and nurtured group of talented professionals who enable my firm to deliver on larger and more complex projects.

There are three overarching benefits of subcontracting for independents. First, business development and engagement management work is done by the agency. They find the work; you fit a need they have. They manage the work; you deliver on the work.

The second big benefit is that there can be less variability in your workflow. Agencies are focused on a continual flow of projects into their pipeline. They look ahead and plan, and often will book their top subcontractors for engagement after engagement after engagement.

The third compelling benefit is that while agency and subcontracting work can provide stability, it also offers flexibility. The choice to take an engagement is totally up to the subcontracted independent. Want to take the summer off? Just say so. Want to carry a heavy load to pay off that new car? Find the engagement that requires lots of hours to complete. Want to work part-time due to family needs? Let the agency know and see if they can find that type of work for you.

Subcontracting can provide a higher degree of security and more regular pay than freelancing, but it does have a few downsides. Subcontractors are still at the whim of the projects that get sold by the firm they are subcontracting for. If the firm is not happy with your work, little work will come your way, no matter what the reason for their discontent. There can be large gaps between projects. There most likely will not be benefits, at least not in the traditional sense. Since you are an independent business hired to do a specific job, you'll have to pay your own employment taxes. You will also not be eligible for unemployment when a project ends.

Of course, there is a price to pay for the value the agency brings. Agencies do the work of matching talent to opportunities and then coordinating and managing the work. The concept is fairly simple. The market rate for your services less the markup of the agency equals the rate you'll receive. If the market rate for your services is $100 per hour and the agency marks up labor by 33 percent, you'll be paid $67 per hour.

I still remember my chagrin when I would invoice Ageos at two-thirds of my direct-to-client billable rate when it seemed like I was the one doing all the work. It was only after I fully understood the work involved in finding a client, landing an engagement, contracting, and then managing that engagement, did I realize that the 33 percent markup was indeed worth it. Ageos had done some very heavy lifting and important work in securing the engagement. I was only doing one part of the overall job, the delivery. Recognizing that doing the work is only a part, albeit an important part, of consulting, I understood the value of subcontracting.

There are a few other considerations that can weigh into your decision to subcontract or go it totally alone. For me, one huge consideration is the amount of autonomy I have to plan the work, deliver the work, and manage the engagement. The short answer is that you have less control as a subcontractor. If autonomy is important to you, then subcontracting may be challenging. For me, that is huge. I found myself chafing when some organizations forbade me from sharing the fact that I had my own consultancy or when they provided a great deal of oversight to my work.

On the flip side, I have a group of trusted peers whom I will offer my services as a subcontractor at the drop of a hat. I may not have created the plan, but I can weigh in. I follow the lead of my contracting peer, but our relationship is such that my advice is often sought.

The final consideration may be the sensitivity of your work and the degree of risk you open yourself to in your practice. If you are designing nuclear power plants, you may well want to have a larger organization that you contract with, as they will bear the cost of the liability insurance and most of the bigger risks.

To summarize, working as a subcontractor is a great way to have a steadier income stream. It also avoids the effort and time involved in finding and managing work and can offset some of the work-related risks you could incur.

Independent Consulting Practice

The choice I made when going independent was to establish my own branded practice, Evergreen Leadership. Katie McNamee and I did the same when we cofounded LEAP .

Professionals that choose this path both run the business and do the work within the business. We are small-business people who sell into a marketplace, and the services we sell are our professional services. We have brands and logos and websites—all created and maintained under our direction. We network and market and propose and sell—and then deliver on the engagements.

Some independent consulting practices are micro, providing employment for only the principal. Others might be run like a small business, employing up to 100 other consultants and perhaps a small administrative staff. These are often called "boutique" consulting practices because it typically targets a narrow specialty or service offering. These firms may be more limited geographically, although that is quickly changing as technology makes it easier and easier to do business virtually, from wherever you are.

Chris Sieber describes small independents as "mice" scurrying under the feet of the elephants, or the behemoth consultancies (Sieber 2009). The good news about being small is that it enables firms to be nimble. We also have less overhead, which is reflected in our pricing structures. Additionally, firms that engage with small independents will find a refreshing change. For their investment, they are dealing with an experienced professional rather than a junior staff member.

This path combines the freedom of freelancing but with a more solid presence in the marketplace. There is the opportunity to build a brand and to engage in bigger projects since you have a structure that enables you to assemble a team. Organizations may be more inclined to contract with you since you present a nice alternative between freelancers and the Big Four. And because this is what I know best, this book is focused primarily on this type of independent career choice.

This choice is heavy on autonomy and choice. The price you pay for that, as Michael Gerber says in his classic book The E-Myth, is that you'll have to develop a proficiency for running a small business and all that entails. Or as Gerber is famous for saying, "working on the business and working in the business." That means you will split your time between business development and client delivery (Gerber 2004).

In the rest of the book, I'll explore in more detail the pros and cons of this approach to an independent career.

Thought Leader

The fourth category of independent professionals includes those individuals who develop a "following" or platform. Freelancers primarily have a specific skill set they sell into the market. Independent consultants typically have broader and deeper expertise as well as the wherewithal to find and manage engagements. Thought leaders have unique and helpful intellectual property that they sell. Think about Stephen Covey and his seven habits or Seth Godin and marketing or Tim Ferris and the four-hour work week.

Thought leaders cut across fields; I suspect that no matter what your profession, there are a few "names" that come to mind as cutting edge, respected professionals. Some have national or international recognition, but many may be more regional or niche. The key question is: do you have a unique and compelling model that helps people frame and address a problem they want to resolve? Do you have intellectual property that you have created and own? Do you have something that the market needs, wants, and is willing to pay for?

Thought leaders disseminate their thoughts in a variety of ways: speaking, writing, coaching, training, or workshops. They are, like freelancers or consultants, paid for their expertise and time. The big difference is that they command a higher fee for their speech, their workshop, or their time. Additionally, they also are likely to have passive income streams from the sales of books or online courses.

For many, there is some appeal to having this type of name recognition. For a few, it may be recognition and fame. My experience is that most are just wildly passionate about their subject and/or approach and feel the calling to disseminate their work. This is the pinnacle of independence—combining professional work you are passionate about with the ability to up your earning prowess. Thought leadership can move professionals beyond selling time for money; instead, the exchange is expertise for money.

While it can become a lucrative path, it is certainly not an easy one. It requires skills in creating unique intellectual property with a fair degree of marketing savvy. Since thought leaders typically write books and blogs or speak and teach, excellent communication skills are required.

We won't discuss thought leaders in greater detail in this book. However, I wanted to mention this opportunity as you take ownership of your career.

A Short Summary

Professionals who choose to work outside traditional employee roles have a number of ways they can do it. Each way brings its own upside and downside. The chart below highlights some of the differences and trade-offs.

	Freelance	Subcontract	Independent Practice	Thought Leader
Control	High	Med	High	High
Flexibility	High	Med	High	High
Autonomy	High	Med	High	High
Limits to Earning Potential	The hours you work	The work the agency sends your way	The market rate for your work	The size & interest of your platform
Choose the work you do	High	Med	High	High
Choose the people you work with	High	Low	High	Med

What Does This Mean for You?

➜ What is appealing to me about working independently?

➜ Based on what I know about myself, which structure(s) would be a good starting place for me?

- Freelancer

- Subcontractor

- Independent Consultant

- Thought Leader

➜ Do I see myself, after getting started, moving to a different structure?

CHAPTER 6

WHAT IT TAKES TO BE A SUCCESSFUL INDEPENDENT

I've painted all the wonderful reasons that many talented professionals are drawn to independent consulting, which makes me wonder who would NOT want to do this. In fact, as I've shared, most of the successful independents I know (and I know quite a few) joke that they are "unemployable" since going back to being an employee would be terribly difficult. That's not to say that it is all rainbows and unicorns. In the following chapters, I'll share some of the common challenges and pitfalls that plague independents.

Trust me. It is absolutely true that being an independent professional is not for everyone. Some of us thrive in this career choice and others thrash around until finally realizing that their talents are better served in a different environment. In fact, most professionals will continue to work in full-time jobs and more traditional employment environments, and that will be the absolute best choice for them. Many will do both by spending a considerable amount of time working for others before working for themselves. And some, like Marion Cook who helped me get started, sandwiched a ten-year independent practice between two longer-term employment stints.

If you are considering independence, I encourage you to take a hard look at your life, your skill set, and your personality traits. This chapter will give you some criteria to consider. You may find that you lack a specific skill or skills, which is not uncommon. I certainly did. The question then becomes—is this something I can fix? And then, is this something I want to fix? Only you can decide.

Five Must-Haves for Independents

In the last three years at LEAP, I've worked closely with professionals who have the desire to be independent. As a result, I get to see the ones who successfully establish themselves and those who don't.

Let me share five of the most common characteristics I see in the professionals who fall into the "successful" column.

1. Marketable Skills

This is basic, very basic. You must, absolutely must, have a skill set that clients are willing to pay for. Not only must they be willing to pay for it, but they must be willing to pay enough for your services that you can make a living from your work. There must also be enough clients who are willing to pay for what you have to offer that you can build a sustainable practice.

You may be lucky enough to have a "hot skill set" and find your skills in high demand. For example, if you are currently an expert in big data, cybersecurity, artificial intelligence, blockchain, online marketing, or the new tax code (to name a few), you have marketable skills. There are also tried and true consulting services that, while not trendy, can provide steady work and income. These include finance and accounting, marketing, human resources, project management, operations, nonprofit governance, and sales management.

As a potential independent professional, one of your first steps should be to assess the market for your skill set, paying particular attention to your level of proficiency. For example, there is currently a solid market for marketing professionals in the online space. However, there is a world of difference between the demand for a professional who creates tweets and LinkedIn posts and the professional who can design and execute a comprehensive social media marketing campaign (which requires more knowledge and expertise).

The good news is that it has never been easier to assess both demand and market price. Google to the rescue! Remember all those sites from chapter five that freelancers use? Spend some time on them in your area of expertise. Who is providing similar services? Who is looking to hire someone with a skill set similar to yours? What are the going rates? Where are potential clients located? In other words, know what the market needs and how you can deliver on it.

Supplement your online search by having conversations with others in your field who are doing what you've set your sights on. What is their assessment of the market? Where are they finding clients? What kind of demand do they have for their services? While these questions may sound intrusive, most people love to talk about what they do and are glad to help others. Be clear that you are considering this as a career option. If they are defensive or put off, move on to someone else who is more helpful.

The final place you can do some market sleuthing is through professional associations associated with your field. Chances are that through these associations you can meet others offering their services as independents. Study the services they offer and the way they present themselves to clients. See if you can find wage and salary surveys. Look for workshops and sessions geared to independents in your field.

There are a few warning signs that your skill set is not as marketable as you would like. Here are the top ones and some examples:

- Your skill set is dated.

  Remember in chapter one how quickly skills can become obsolete today? You may be a world-class expert, but if your specialty is in an area or on a platform that is not very relevant or is dated (such as Perl, Adobe Flash & Air, or .net), then your opportunities diminish.

- Your skill set is very narrow.

Oftentimes, companies will take their best performers and develop them into super subject matter experts (SuperSMEs) for proprietary or company-specific equipment, systems, or processes. When I worked at a print shop, we had custom-developed ERP systems, custom-designed equipment, and proprietary inventory control processes. Our best and brightest were often those who could troubleshoot the thorniest problem lickety-split. The problem is that no other company had anything comparable.

- Your skill set is too broad.

I see this problem with people who have great generalist skills. As a result, they are often moved from project to project as an integral, all-purpose team player. These are professionals who are reliable, dependable, and willing to do what it takes. Often, they learn quickly and get along with a variety of people. But what they lack is a specific defined skill set. One person with this problem struggled to describe what he would do for a client. After much thought, he came up with "integrate people, process, and technology." Trouble is, I've yet to see a client look for that specific skill set.

- You are too green.

I can still vividly recall the conversation I had with a sincere Purdue student of mine. Jack (name changed to avoid embarrassment) had been a top student in my consulting course. We had met at a local coffee shop to discuss some ideas from class. After we had our coffees and chitchatted for a bit, he got to the heart of it all. He had been so inspired by the course that he wanted to go independent as well. From what I had seen that semester, he was smart, organized, and had good communication skills—all good qualities for doing this. It was when I asked what his service offering would be that my heart dropped, and I scrambled to gather my thoughts. He wanted to coach leaders in small businesses. He liked the ability to influence. He thought they could use his help. The big problem that he was unable to see was that he had never started or led a small business. Outside of a class project team, he had never led others. He was too green.

Many of us might fall into the "Jack" trap. We get a glimpse of someone doing something we think is interesting or intriguing or fun, and we fantasize about being that person or doing that work. We want to skip the step of the grunt work that it takes to do the work we want to help others do. Or we decide to become instant experts by signing up for the certification or course or reading a few books. Just as I had to tell Jack, I'll tell you: Until you have done it, and done it well, you will be hard-pressed to sell your services as an expert in the market. A course alone does not make you an expert, only time in the trenches does. There are many ways we can work towards that dream. We can take a course. We can ask our employers for opportunities to use those skills. We can get a job in the field. We can volunteer our services at a nonprofit that would benefit from our skills and learn at the same time. But, at the end of the day, you have to put in your hours. You need to actually be able to do what you are advising or guiding others to do.

- You are only mediocre.

This brings me to my final point. You not only need to have done it; you need to have done it consistently well. I am not telling you that you have to be perfect, that is an unattainable state. But you do need to be good at what you do—for multiple reasons. Clients hire consultants and pay a premium to get top skills. The pressure to perform and to perform quickly comes with this career, and you can do neither if you are muddling through. Additionally, for most people, there is more joy doing something at which they are excellent. Work quickly becomes sheer drudgery when you are merely passable at it.

2. Self-Starter

The transition to independent consultant fascinates me and would be an interesting study in human behavior. I've worked with many professionals who talk about their desire to begin independent professional work. But there is a marked delineation between those who are ready to take action and those who are not.

Without a doubt, the transition pace can vary widely. Some choose to move quickly and others more methodically, setting up a step-by-step exit plan from employment to independence. Yet no matter the pace, those who make it go quickly beyond talking about it and start doing something about it. They share the trait of being a self-starter.

> Self-starters are the professionals who do the work they need to do, even if there are a million other things that demand their attention. They are the people who don't wait for direction; instead, they create their own direction. They carry on even when they are tired, discouraged, or tempted to take a nap.

Self-starters are the professionals who do the work they need to do, even if there are a million other things that demand their attention. They are the people who don't wait for direction; instead, they create their own direction. They carry on even when they are tired, discouraged, or tempted to take a nap.

They get up, walk down the hall to their home office, and put their time in, even when they don't have clients yet or deadlines associated with an engagement. They don't need a boss telling them what to do. They are their own boss. They are the resilient individuals who pick themselves up when a potential client says no and immediately begin seeking the next opportunity.

Again, I want to stress that it is not speed but diligence that differentiates those who are successful in the long run. Read through again the stories of April Petrey, Karl Riddett, or Alexandra Rufatto-Perry. At some point, I predict that each of these talented professionals will seem like an overnight success. I know differently.

Each has put in many years of careful preparation to lay the groundwork for launching their practices. For some, that foundation involves skill building. For others, it involves developing a strong professional network. And, for other self-starters, it means amassing a financial nest egg and slashing expenses to get through the start-up phase.

What all this means is that "owning it" means "working it." You'll need to prepare, do the work, and show up—without a boss, with self-imposed deadlines, and with an eye to a better future, even if you are not exactly certain what that is going to be.

3. Like Variety

As I look at this subhead, I wonder if the right descriptor is not "likes variety," but "craves variety." No matter. Being independent appeals to others like me, who get bored easily. As I talk to successful independents, many report having a touch of ADD or at least a propensity to enjoy the challenge of learning and executing on a broad set of skills.

If you are a person who thrives in an environment of stability and likes predictable routines and being fully prepared and on top of things, let the idea of being an independent pass over you like a wave on the shore. Variety, uncertainty, and continually adapting to weird and wonderful situations are the day-to-day realities of being independent.

> If you are a person who thrives in an environment of stability and likes predictable routines and being fully prepared and on top of things, let the idea of being an independent pass over you like a wave on the shore.

The reality of running a small business AND doing the work you're billing for contributes mightily to the variety you get every day. My typical day bounces from entering expenses in QuickBooks (boring but necessary) to leading a live webinar to outlining a proposal for a new client to having a coaching conversation to sending out invoices—all before noon.

Running a small business means you do pretty much everything. It requires that you set up an organizational infrastructure (accounting, taxes, business organization, etc.), develop marketing plans, coordinate selling, manage contracts, and execute on the engagement. Any one of those categories would keep you busy, and, as owner, you're going to have to be at least conversant in all of them. Some of these tasks you may be able to outsource (assuming you have the income), but there is no avoiding the hard fact that marketing, selling, and delivering the work is up to you.

In addition to the variety of tasks required to keep the business going, there are plenty of other sources of variety in a small business. No matter how standardized your service offerings are, each and every client is different. What works for one client may bomb with the next. Client situations also change. I've had the leaders who sponsored our work leave the organization. I've also had projects that were fully funded and going swimmingly, only to have the funding pulled and a two-year project jettisoned in two weeks.

And finally, as we mentioned in chapter one, the body of knowledge in your area of expertise is continually and quickly changing. It is up to you to stay current by keeping your skills sharp and continually upgrading what you offer. Clients hire you for your skills, and the expectations are high. Stay sharp to stay employed.

4. Entrepreneurially Minded

Remember my earlier story about my first venture into starting something? In my early thirties, my friend, Carmen, and I had a big dream. We wanted to create high-quality, affordable childcare run by well-trained and well-paid staff where parents were an integral part of their child's experience. Being young and optimistic, and not knowing what we didn't know, we thought we were the perfect people to do this big thing.

We articulated our vision and formed a company. We did this as a side hustle, while both of us worked our regular, more than full-time jobs on top of raising our own children. And ... we did it! Well, we did some of it. We founded two award-winning employer childcare centers that still exist today and also opened after-school programs and summer camps. What we didn't do was find a good way to make the business financially sustainable.

The long-lasting outcome for me was that this desire to create something tangible out of a dream persisted. I learned that I could build something of value. I could take some measured risks, and I liked being my own boss.

When I exited the business in 1988, I vowed to myself that I would start something else again. I didn't know what or how or when, but I knew I would. It took another sixteen years before I did it. It was when I went out on my own as an independent consultant by launching K. Taylor & Associates LLC.

Many other independent consultants have that same urge, that itch to start something of their own. Some have explored other ways to scratch that entrepreneurial itch. Alana Robinson bought into a franchise and then turned to independent consulting to earn enough income to cover the losses incurred in the franchise. Along the way, she realized that independent consulting was a much better fit for her than operating a franchise.

It doesn't matter if your entrepreneurial itch is as itchy as an outbreak after an encounter with poison ivy or just a twinge now and then, the idea of creating, launching, managing, and growing your own company must, on some level, hold a fair amount of appeal to you. If it doesn't, the ups and downs, the slow months, the crazy overloaded months, and the uncertainty that accompanies being a business owner will cause you to run full tilt back to using your skills as an employee.

For remember, even though you can design your business around the work that you are good at and passionate about, you still have to be a good enough business person to make it a go.

The good news is that how to run a business is a learned skill. Here are some quick questions that will help you sort out if you have what it takes to be entrepreneurially minded:

- Do you generate ideas about how things could be better or different, or how problems could be solved?

- Are you able to execute on those ideas?

- Can you take a measured risk?

- Can you rebound from missteps and failures?

- Do you have the drive to succeed in spite of obstacles?

- Are you able to learn quickly?

- Are you able to persevere when things get tough?

Trust that you can learn to market, sell, and do the accounting. Trust that you can figure out how to create a business plan and craft a clear value proposition. And also trust your personal assessment of your desire to start and operate a small business. If it excites you, proceed. If it makes you want to throw up, think again.

5. Resilient

People tell me all the time that they really want to do what I do. Trouble is, they don't know exactly what I do. Here is what they think my work life is like:

- Get up whenever the urge strikes me

- Spend office time in my PJs

- Work on exciting engagements

- Have people admire me for my brilliance

- Make a lot of money

- Work whenever the urge strikes me, but somewhere in the neighborhood of 20 or 30 hours per week

This is closer to reality:

- Get up at 6 a.m.

- Write and create IP until 8 or 9 a.m.

- Work hard to deliver the best I can for a variety of clients—each different, some difficult, and most all who have priorities other than working with me

- Influence some people positively some of the time

- Work based on client demands, which might mean long days or weekends in busy times

- Make a good living if I am diligent about minding my pipeline and my expenses

Have no doubt. I would not change my work and my life for anything. But there is a grittiness and resilience that one must bring to this work. That includes the ability to continue to sell, even after you've heard fifteen nos. The willingness to stay with a potential client over time, sometimes years, with patience until they are finally ready to get that contract in place. The ability to put forth your best ideas in a proposal and then hold your head high when that work goes to someone else based on price. The strength to set straight a project that has gone sideways, often due to nothing you have done.

Yes, I do have moments in the spotlight, and deep satisfaction when I see, proof positive, that my work has made a positive difference. And I've made a great living doing this. I am able to reap those benefits by staying with it, doing the work, and continually learning and sharpening my skills. I do these things because I am resilient and because it is worth it.

A Short Summary

Launching, successfully running, and building an individual consultancy is not for everyone. It may be for you if these things describe you:

- Have marketable skills
- Are a self-starter
- Like variety
- Are entrepreneurially minded
- Are resilient

What Does This Mean for You?

Think about each of these success factors. Where are you strong? Where are your challenge areas?

➜ Do I have a marketable skill set?

➜ Am I entrepreneurially minded?

➜ Do I thrive in an environment with continual variety?

➜ Am I a self-starter?

➜ Am I resilient enough to stick with something when it gets hard?

Reflect on the areas that are challenging for you.

➜ Which ones are fixable?

➜ What would you need to do to fix them?

➜ Are you willing to take the time and make the effort to fix them?

CHAPTER 7

WARNING: THIS PATH IS NOT FOR EVERYONE

In the last chapter, I shared some indicators that running your own business as an independent professional might be for you. In this chapter, I'll share six warning signs that should cause you to proceed with caution.

As I left my employer, I was not the only one who decided they would make a go of independent consulting. Only a few of us have made it. Most of that aspiring group did not. Some found it was not for them. Others made some strategic and tactical errors. A few fled quickly back to the perceived safety of full-time/regular employment.

Starting to freelance or launching a consultancy is not for everyone, and it is clearly not for the faint of heart. The statistics tell the story. According to the U.S. Bureau of Labor Statistics, approximately 20 percent of small businesses fail in the first year, and only 50 percent survive to year five. Those numbers continue to diminish with only 35 percent of firms surviving long enough to celebrate their tenth year in business (SBA 2012). While I don't have specific numbers for consultancies compared to other small businesses, I have no reason to believe that we are any less prone to failure.

The possibility of failing aside, your personal investment in time, energy, focus, and money (yes, it will take money to get started) is not insignificant. The decision to go independent is a big one, and you want to go into it sober and clear eyed. The decision NOT to go independent can be, for many, a rock-solid decision.

As I share some warning signs, I'll also divulge which of these problems are permanent and which can be either mitigated or overcome. All are presented with the belief that it is far better to know about potential problems and how to overcome them before you take the big step to consulting. A delay to better position yourself can be time well spent. And remember the lessons of April Petrey, Karl Riddett, and Alexandra Ruffatto-Perry—they are shining examples of taking your time to do it right.

Seven Warning Signs That This May NOT Be for You

1. Lack of Verifiable Credentials

If you recall, the very first criteria for success was having up-to-date, relevant, and marketable skills, but here is the kicker. You have to be able to verify that you can actually do what you say you can do.

Think about it. When you go to the doctor, all those certificates on the wall reassure you that you are in good hands. Your local mechanic may proudly display their Better Business Bureau accreditation. Before you hand over the keys to your house to a carpenter, you ask for references.

Businesses vetting professionals for important work that needs to get done and for which they are going to pay a nice amount of money want the same reassurances before they turn over the keys to their business. And so, as an independent, you need to have ways to "prove it."

For many, verifiable credentials are issued by an objective body that has validated your skill set. This may be a degree from a reputable school, or perhaps certification from a professional organization which requires you to pass a knowledge exam and/or a practicum. Other examples include obtaining your CPA, passing the law boards, or being granted an SHRM certification. You might be Microsoft certified in certain IT skills, or you might invest in a coaching certification. If you are a project manager, having your PMP is helpful.

If you have certifications, be certain that you find places to let others know that you have them. They can be added to your LinkedIn profile, added to your resume or bio, placed on your website, or noted on your business card.

It may be that you don't have degrees or certifications, either because they don't exist in your field of expertise or because you've not had the opportunity to obtain them. If that is the case, you'll have to find other ways to assure potential clients that you are reputable and can do what you say you can do.

References and testimonials are powerful ways to do this. Having someone else sing your praises is far better than you blathering on about how wonderful and smart you are. Just having a list of references with contact information is a credibility builder. When people see my list of references and past clients, they sometimes follow through and reach out to those listed. Sometimes they don't, but you still send the message that you have others who will vouch for you. And who is on the list matters greatly.

LinkedIn is a great way to capture endorsements and recommendations. Identify those who know you, know the quality of your work, and can speak with authority about both. Selecting individuals with similar job titles as the people who will likely hire you as an independent is another good strategy; they lend far more credibility than your third-grade teacher.

It may be that your work product is such that you can use it to establish credibility. Can you create a portfolio? A listing of projects with key success metrics? Blogs or LinkedIn posts that demonstrate your prowess? For many professionals, particularly those who want to establish themselves as thought leaders, speaking engagements and/or writing a book is a great way to demonstrate professional skills.

No matter your tactic, answer the question of how a potential client could validate that you have the skills and abilities they want to hire you for. If you have verifiable credentials, get them in order and place them front and center. If you don't, this is one of those areas that is fixable. Get that degree, obtain the certification, assemble your portfolio, write that white paper, or speak at a relevant professional association. You may be brilliant, but potential clients will want to trust AND verify.

2. No Financial Safety Net

Okay, this is a big one—a very big one—and here is why. Freelance and consulting income is erratic. There are no regular paychecks. You may begin with a client in hand (many of us have), or you may have to scramble for months to land that first engagement. And that first engagement may be large and lucrative, or it may only be getting your big toe in the door.

I suspect you are shaking your head up and down and thinking that you know this. Here are three things you may not know that amplify the erratic nature of getting paid for consulting and freelance work.

1. There can be a long time between getting the engagement and getting a paycheck. Let's say you've spent month one in the proposal and vetting process. The work begins in month two. You invoice at the beginning of month three. They pay net 60 (and some big firms pay net 90). By the time that money appears in your bank account, it has taken four to six months, even though you have an agreement and have been delivering on the work.

2. The time between the initial conversation with a potential client and being hired to do actual work can be excruciatingly long. Granted, there are times that I've landed a nice engagement after just a few meetings and a few weeks. There are also times that it has taken years (and I am not exaggerating) to move from initial conversation to consulting engagement. And even more common is that it may take four to six weeks to move a contract through internal procurement processes, even after you have an agreed-upon proposal and a client with a budget.

3. Sometimes clients just don't pay. At times, this is because you got lost in accounts payable, end up in procurement purgatory, or have to start over. Other times, it is because they are dealing with their own cash flow issues, and as a small player, you don't have the leverage other suppliers do to move up in the queue. And every once in a while, it is because they just can't, due to bankruptcy or severe financial crisis.

I once had a coaching conversation with a professional who desperately wanted to freelance but didn't have enough money to put gas in her car. My advice to her was direct and simple: Get a job. Get a job right now and save your money until you have some financial cushion.

The amount of safety net needed depends on any number of factors:

- How much do you have in savings?

- How liquid is that money?

- How much money do you need to pay for the basics?

- What other sources of income do you have?

- Are there others who depend on you and who will not be excited about eating ramen noodles some weeks?

- How good are you at managing the money you do have?

- Where are the places that you can slash expenses to reduce your need for income?

- What expenses will you have to get your business up and running?

- How long do you anticipate it will take you to find engagements?

I would encourage you to cut expenses to the core and have some type of safety net—a minimum of six months. See if you can put in place some type of supplemental income to help you bridge the gap between a regular paycheck and those first consulting checks.

On one extreme, some would say not to venture into independent consulting until you have five years' worth of a safety net. I, personally, think that is not only excessive but unrealistic for most.

I would encourage you to cut expenses to the core and have some type of safety net—a minimum of six months. See if you can put in place some type of supplemental income to help you bridge the gap between a regular paycheck and those first consulting checks.

For me, a six-month severance package gave me the safety net to start. It allowed me enough time to test whether my idea would work. Since I was able to begin quickly with client engagement, I stashed money into savings until I was truly confident that I could make a go of it.

Once again, I will say to you that a financial base is fixable. And, once again, I advise you not to jump into consulting until it is fixed. Only you can determine the safety net you'll need but do the work and create one. It will give you the freedom to focus on growing your business and the fortitude to say no to undesirable client work for the sake of a paycheck.

3. Health Constraints

As you contemplate going out on your own, there are two health-related factors you need to grapple with. The first is your own health, and the second is your ability to access health care.

Ask any small business owner, and they will tell you: there are no sick or PTO days. As a small business owner, not only will you not get paid if you are sick, but the likelihood is very high that there is no one else to step in and do the work. While each of us is prone to a bout of the flu or the sniffles, if you are someone who takes frequent time off for health reasons, I'd encourage you to consider how your current health status might impact your commitments to clients and your earning potential.

Some questions to consider include:

- How frequently am I too ill to work?

- How much ability will I have to schedule health appointments?

- How flexible will my client work be?

- How much of my client work will be delivered on-site or face-to-face?

- How time-sensitive is my work? Will a delay from a health issue be a big problem for my potential clients?

The second health-related factor you'll need to solve is how to access health insurance. I wish I had a great solution for you, but alas, I do not. For myself, as well as my peers, we find creative ways to cover health insurance that include:

- Having coverage from a spouse or partner

- Having coverage through your parents (if you are young enough) or Medicare (if you are old enough)

- Having coverage as part of a pension program through yourself, spouse, or partner

- Working a part-time job that provides health care

- Using COBRA as a bridge between employment and your self-employment plan

- Sourcing health care on the open market

Before you make the decision to go independent, know what your health care coverage plan will be. Be prepared for sticker shock if you step into the markets, especially if you've had the good fortune to be with an employer who heavily subsidized the cost of insurance. I've found that a good insurance broker can walk you through possible choices and help you make the best decision for your circumstances.

I wish this was different. I wish I could tell you that you'll find the right answer, and it will stay that way. I suspect that how you access health care coverage will change over time. It certainly has for me. I've moved from COBRA to being covered by my husband's retirement plan to purchasing on the open market to being covered via a part-time job to COBRA and then to Medicare. All of these changes are exactly why warning sign #4 made the list!

4. Inability to Deal with Ambiguity

Ambiguity abounds in the independent consultant's world. In fact, there may be more unknowns than knowns. For those starting out, there is uncertainty about making a go of this, uncertainty about what services to offer and whom to offer them to, uncertainty about how to describe yourself and your services, and uncertainty about how to let the right people know you are available for hire.

All that uncertainty begins to fade away as you find your way. You will get through all of this but not without some adjustments. You will figure out if this will work or not, and you'll find how to position yourself in the market.

You might think that is the end of it, but it is only the beginning. When the first potential client asks you for a proposal, you may see ten different ways to approach it. You'll have to wade through that murkiness to arrive at the client site with a great proposal. If it's accepted, you may even think that all is good, but what faces you is even more ambiguity.

Once you begin the work, you'll quickly find that the problem you've been asked to help solve will either be different than described, harder than anticipated, or even more likely, not the real problem at all. The people you need to count on to implement your project have competing priorities, and you're not even sure you are on the list. Your tried and true ten-step process to project success flounders at step four. The scope changes and players move on and off the team. The client is looking to you for direction, and you are feeling pretty clueless. Welcome to the world of professional consulting.

There are no perfect clients. There are no perfect engagements. There are no perfect consultants. But there are some who are better than others. These are the consultants who can flex without compromising their core values. They can observe, ask good questions, win trust, listen hard, and propose approaches and solutions on the fly. They are the ones who stay super focused on the desired outcome of the engagement and find creative ways to achieve the goal.

If you do best in predictable environments, take note. If you derive great satisfaction when things run like clockwork, carry on with your current employer. If you abhor uncertainty and can't function in chaos, find a different occupation. Independent consulting is not for you. And this is one of the warning indicators that is not fixable. Repeat: NOT FIXABLE

5. Difficulty Making Decisions Alone

Independent consultants are making decisions all the time. Decisions that impact their practice like:

- How much should I charge for my services?

- How do I price this proposal?

- What is the best approach for this engagement?

- Do I need a webpage?

- What PC do I purchase?

- Is this a client I want to do work with?

Even more unsettling, at least for me, are the decisions that impact my clients:

- How much latitude do I have to speak hard truths?

- What is the best approach?

- How do I get the right people involved?

- How do I help my client lessen their dependence on me?

- What are the most helpful recommendations I can make?

- How do I ensure the solutions we put in place remain long past my engagement?

- What is the most important work to do with this client right now?

Most of the time, these are decisions you are making alone. It is your business, and you can seek advice, but the final decision is yours. It is your client and your engagement, and yes, you can reach out to trusted peers to brainstorm options. But at the end of the day, you own this engagement, this client, and this outcome.

As with most skills, the more practice you get, the more patterns emerge, and the more alert you are to warning signs. You learn as you go, and while decisions may not get much easier, you at least can make more informed decisions and avoid past mistakes.

I can clearly recall spending over 40 hours in four days, pulling together my very first proposal for my brand. It was a proposal for just north of $50K, and I agonized. I did the financials over and over again. I estimated the time, then added time for good measure because I thought I had underestimated. I then turned around and reduced the hours because I thought the proposal was overpriced. And then I rewrote and edited it one more time, just in case.

While it would be excessive now, all that thinking and working and rewriting and recalculating helped me learn to see the patterns, and I started to figure out what factors were critical. I was able to find the words that the client would understand and respond to.

I continue to ask the same questions as I prepare each and every proposal I write now:

- What does success look like?

- Are we solving the right problem?

- Have I left anything out?

- What if I overestimated? Underestimated?

- Is this fair to the client? Is it fair to me?

- Would I be happy to do this work at the price I quoted even if I severely underestimated it?

The difference between when I started out and now is my speed and confidence. I can write similar proposals in hours, not days. The quality of the proposal is not a reflection of the time I spend, but the quality of thought I put into it. And the quality of our thinking improves with practice and feedback. In my case, the feedback that helped me grow is real-world, really-matters feedback.

Yet even though I am better at it, actually much better at it, I still experience a pang of panic when I hit send, for I know I've just made some very big decisions—all alone and by myself.

If making decisions all by yourself is a problem area, you might be well served to think about different approaches to doing this type of work. You might not set up your own consulting practice but might instead consider joining a small consulting team. You might subcontract. You might start a side hustle to test your comfort level and develop confidence in your decision-making capabilities. In other words, proceed carefully. Proceed very carefully with this challenge area.

6. Weak Network

I can still vividly recall my network during the time immediately post RR Donnelley. I had my newly printed business card with my fresh logo, cool stationery, and stamps. I was ready to announce my new firm to the world. The problem was this: my world was small, pathetically small. I bought 50 stamps and had some left over. My network was also pathetically narrow. Ninety-five percent of those on the list were coworkers (or past coworkers) from my employer. The remaining five percent was my family and friends.

Believe me when I say that as an independent, your network is one of your biggest assets, second only to having a marketable skill set. In fact, you can have a marketable skill set, and without a network, you will find you have no one to get the word out to. There's no one to connect you with potential clients and, as a result, no work!

Perhaps you are one of those people who think networking is all about passing out lots of business cards to anyone who crosses your path. It is not.

Perhaps you believe that your sheer brilliance and amazing skills will win you work. It will not.

Perhaps you think that networking is a superficial, super waste of time. It is not.

Perhaps you hate networking with a passion, and you think a nice billboard or SEO strategy will enable you to get the word out from the comfort of your couch. It will not.

You need a network. And you need the right network.

The strength of your network is not measured by size alone. Social media enables you to have thousands of LinkedIn connections and just as many Facebook friends.

The real question is not how many, but how many know you? Know what you do? Trust you? Would refer you? Vouch for you? Hire you?

If you don't have a network, you can create one. When I left my employer, my network was comprised primarily of people in the organization where I had worked for the past fourteen years. Luckily for me, I had a variety of roles across the organization, so I did have a broad network, even if it was limited to one company. Even luckier for me was that many of those in this internal network exited from the company at the same time I did. Within six to ten months, they had landed at other companies. By staying in touch with them, my network stretched considerably wider. It was those connections that led me to my first engagements. And those first clients led me to the next ones. And those clients led me to other clients.

To strengthen my puny and pathetic network, I consciously nurtured relationships with a fervor. I knew that strong and trusted **relationships** led to **referrals**. Referrals led to work, and the better my work was, the more likely I would get **repeat business**. My entire marketing strategy was executing on these three R's—relationships, referrals, and repeat business. And it worked.

So clearly, having a weak network falls into the "you can fix this" category if you are willing to put in the time and effort. You can learn to network. Professional or civic organizations are great places to start. Join. Volunteer. Add value.

If you don't have a LinkedIn profile, create one. Think of this as your electronic Rolodex (some of us older folks will know what that means). As you are introduced to people that you would like to have in your network, send them an invitation to connect. This cements them into your network, so that no matter where their career takes them, you are able to reach out to them. And it's less messy than having stacks of business cards on your desk.

Build your network strategically; it is not about volume but quality. You can learn more about the five types of people you'll want in your network by going to Leap's consulting blog.

> Build your network strategically; it is not about volume but quality.

Learn to network. It is an art. Observe those who are good at it. Read a book about it. Practice it. Find the ways that work for you. But do it, because the rewards are rich.

And I'm the poster child for going from a really shaky network to a vibrant one. By the numbers, I have a network of 2,330 on LinkedIn—and these are not just random connections. Numbers aside, I have an amazing group of peers, current clients, past clients, and colleagues who know me, know my work, trust me, and are willing to refer me. My network is one of the biggest blessings that I have in my life—personally and professionally.

7. Unwilling to Promote Yourself or Sell Your Services

I'll admit it, my discomfort with the idea of "selling" caused me great angst in the first five years of my practice. And it still bites me in the butt on occasion. I know that I'm not alone. Many skilled professionals have a fear of selling.

The surface reason for this is the stereotype that we carry about a salesperson working hard (and perhaps even deceiving you) to sell you something you don't need, didn't want, and can't afford. We compare ourselves to the used car salesmen or telemarketers we dread. We associate selling with someone who is way too slick that pressures us (or just wears us down) to open our wallet to buy something we don't need at a price we can't afford.

As professionals, we sell best when we are sincere and not slick. We do best when we are acting for the mutual benefit of our potential clients and ourselves. We know that when we only sell what really helps the client and we walk away from work that is not in their best interest, trust is built that serves us over the long term.

That is a perception we need to move beyond. As professionals, we sell best when we are sincere and not slick. We do best when we are acting for the mutual benefit of our potential clients and ourselves. We know that when we only sell what really helps the client and we walk away from work that is not in their best interest, trust is built that serves us over the long term.

There is an even deeper and more profound reason that selling freelancing or consulting services strikes fear in the hearts of the most competent professionals. It is because we are not selling widgets or timeshares or Girl Scout cookies. We are selling ourselves—our skills and our ability to help a client do some important work or solve a thorny problem.

And so, in our mind, the sale becomes more than the transaction itself. It becomes a referendum on our intrinsic value and worth. And with that, a sale can become personal. Deeply personal.

Add to that the angst that comes with putting a price on your services, and it gets even harder. Believe me, putting a number on the value of your time, your expertise, and your skill set is daunting and surfaces a host of insecurities about who you are, what you deserve, and how much you are worth.

Yet the hard reality is that once you decide to freelance or be independent, you have to sell the work to do the work. It doesn't just happen when your website is up or your LinkedIn profile is spiffed up. You can't outsource this task to someone else.

There is no instant magic fairy dust here, but there is some magic that happens when you work through this. You reach a more psychologically grounded place when you are comfortable selling your services by setting a price that is fair to you and your client and learning to disentangle your ego from the sales process. It's a place where one transaction does not define your overall value and where you are comfortable presenting your services with confidence and not bravado. It's a place where you can seek the best solution for a client rather than the sale for yourself.

Just as with networking, you can learn to do this hard thing with guidance, reflection, work, and practice. The question for you: if selling scares the pants off you, are you willing to do what it takes to get your pants back on and figure this out?

What You Can Fix/What You Cannot

To summarize, going independent is no small decision. The more established you are in your career, the weightier the decision.

I encourage you to take an inventory of both your assets and liabilities (use the checklist at the end of this chapter) and give yourself the gift of honesty. This is not the time to sugarcoat your own skills, abilities, and propensities.

If you come up short in the following categories, I would discourage you from proceeding down the path to independence:

- Not a self-starter
- Being entrepreneurial is not appealing

- Discomfort with ambiguity

- Inability to make decisions quickly with incomplete information

- Unwillingness to do the work to prepare for this career shift

If the things above are not impediments for you, identify the places where you have some work yet to do. Consider where you have barriers, and what can you do to overcome them. What can you do to grow your network? How can you verify your credentials? What can you do to learn about launching a small business? Where can you cut expenses and add to your financial safety net?

Many highly successful independent consultants that I work with created a path to their practices. For some, it was a ten-year journey getting things in place. For others, it took a single year of focused effort. For me, it was without much initial foresight or planning, followed by lots of hard work and learning on the fly. (By the way, this is not the path I'd recommend.)

A Short Summary

Independent consulting has its challenges and is not for everybody. This chapter outlined six areas that can create problems for independents. Some are fixable; some are not. The self-assessment that follows will help you ascertain your current situation. To review, the six potential problems include:

1. Lack of verifiable credentials

2. No financial safety net

3. Health constraints

4. Inability to deal with ambiguity

5. Difficulty making decisions alone

6. Weak network

Assess Where You Stand

This brings us back to the beginning. Are you a self-starter? If yes, then you should take stock of where you are, make a plan, and get started! The self-assessment quiz below can help you self-evaluate where you have strengths, where you have challenges, and where you have some work to do.

Rate each statement on a scale of 1 to 10, with 1 being not at all, 3 being pretty pathetic, 7 being respectable, and 10 being very much so. Once you have done the self-assessment, take a solid look at what you see and reflect on what that means for you and your career.

Guess what? There is not a scoring key that tells you to add up all your numbers or a chart that tells you what they mean. If that makes you uncomfortable, refer to the ability to tolerate ambiguity and to make decisions on your own. This is a case where you are dealing with both!

Self-Assessment	Rating on a scale of 1 (low) to 10 (high)
My professional skills are up to date and applicable to freelancing or consulting.	
The market rate I could charge would enable me to live comfortably.	
There is demand in the market for the skills I possess.	
I am a self-starter.	
I possess the discipline to execute on the plans I create.	
I can work through disappointments and setbacks.	
Having variety in my work energizes me.	
I can stay organized with multiple demands on my time.	
I can set priorities and stay focused on them.	
I can avoid distractions and time wasters.	
The idea of having my own business excites me.	
I either can do or am interested in doing things like simple accounting, marketing, and sales.	
I am motivated by a desire to take control of my schedule, my career, and my life.	
I have clarity about my highest priorities.	
Having flexibility in my work schedule would serve me well.	
I have verifiable credentials that validate the skills I bring.	
I hold relevant degrees and certifications.	

I have a portfolio of my work that I can share with others.

I know the amount of income I'd need to earn to cover my living expenses.

I have enough of a financial safety net to see me through the launching of my practice.

I am able to manage erratic income.

I am able to do good work in situations that are ambiguous.

I can set my own direction and make my own decisions.

I am a quick learner.

I perform well in new situations.

I am able to make decisions quickly, even when I don't have perfect information.

I have a strong network of other professionals who know me and my work and trust me.

What Does This Mean for You?

→ As you review the checklist, what are your key takeaways?

→ What problem areas have you identified?

→ Could these problems be remedied over time with effort?

➡ What warning indicators have you uncovered?

➡ How does that inform your next steps?

CHAPTER 8

10 THINGS TO KNOW BEFORE YOU GO INDEPENDENT

You may, by this point, be eager and anxious to get started. Being independent is something you have dreamed about. You have friends and peers who have done this, and you are envious of their career choice. Yet we all know there is a difference between what you see on the outside and what it is really like on the inside.

In this chapter, I'm going to share with you the things I've found to be true about being independent. Some things are wonderful; others come with the occupation. No career or job or life is perfect, but independent consulting, for me, is as close to perfect as it comes.

Nonetheless, it will be helpful for you to go into this fully informed, rather than discovering unexpected surprises once you're in. These are things that no one shared with me before I started, but it sure would have been helpful if they had.

1. Client Delivery Is Your First Priority ... But Not Your Only One

One of the primary reasons I chose to go independent was to do more of the work I loved. And while that has certainly worked for me, I've been startled by the amount of time it takes to find the clients that have the work that you love and then to work the process of getting an agreement to do that work.

If you envision independent consulting as working with a client doing really important work and working for hours in sheer bliss, then know that you will have some days where this will happen.

You'll also have days (or weeks) when you are not doing client work (a.k.a., paid work). You will be laying the groundwork, you'll spend time searching for clients that need your good work, and you'll be meeting with potential clients about how your good work might help do something important for them. Hopefully, you'll also be writing proposals and spending time executing contracts and putting together reports and invoices.

Here are my two biggest insights that I'd like to share with you on this topic:

1. The amount of time you spend "on your business" will vary, but there will always be some time you need to dedicate to this. Exactly how much time it will take depends on several factors:

> The amount of time you spend "on your business" will vary, but there will always be some time you need to dedicate to this.

- How established are you?

- How in demand are your services?

- How aptly have you set up ways to keep your pipeline of potential work filled?

In the beginning, I spent 80 percent of my time building the business, and only 20 percent of my time delivering work for clients. With time, that started to shift. There are windows now where I have had several large, long-term projects and the percentages flip: I'll spend most of my time on client delivery and 20 percent on the business. The key takeaway remains the same—the choice to be independent also means the need to run your business.

2. On my daily to-do list, client work (and doing it well) is my top priority. I can't afford to let due dates slip. I can't sustain my practice if I do shoddy work, as my reputation is critical. Yet it cannot be my only priority. The classic problem that independents have is the inability to find a balance between business delivery and business development. This manifests itself as a boom/bust cycle. There may be months in which the independent is heads down and totally focused on client work. The project ends, and there is nothing in the pipeline. The independent shifts gears and is heads down and totally focused on finding the next engagement. It comes, and the focus shifts to 100 percent on client delivery again. It ends, and there is no work to replace it, and so it starts all over again. So, while the delivery of client work is your top priority, it should not be your only priority. There are ways to keep a steady flow in the pipeline—and the time you spend setting up those systems is well worth it.

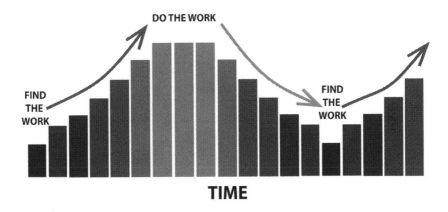

I did a tally of how I spent my time during eleven months of the past year, classifying time into three buckets:

1. Client time (billable time)

2. Business time (marketing, books, networking, investing in myself)

3. Personal time (vacation, holiday, personal time)

This was not an easy task since many days are spent doing a bit of all three. In North Carolina, I might get up and blog, run a few coaching calls, coordinate a networking meeting, and then head to the beach. Even though there is a touch of imprecision, the breakdown for my past year looked like this (excluding weekends and holidays):

- 107 days of client time (44%)
- 74 days of business time (31%)
- 60 days of "my" time (25%)

For me, this is a great picture of what you can build with consistent work and focus. In this same year, my total sales were just south of $200K, which was neither my best year nor my worst. I delivered some great client work, continued to devote time to growing my business (we started LEAP in this year), and still enjoyed free time (most of which I spent in North Carolina on the beach).

2. Your Network Is an Asset: Treat It Accordingly

Second only to your skill set is the value of your network. I can guarantee that if two consultants have equal skill and experience, the one with the better network is going to outshine the other—hands down.

Here is why. Hiring an independent is most often done by referral. One businessperson with a need reaches out to someone they trust and asks, "Who do you know who can help me with xyz ...?" And so, the more people who know and trust you, the more referrals you are likely to get. The fact that you were referred by a trusted source gives you an edge on anyone who comes up as the result of a Google search.

Networking (and the resulting network) is **not** any of these things:

- Passing out hundreds of business cards to casual acquaintances
- Pressuring people to pass your name along to others
- Adding hundreds of names to your LinkedIn connections just to hit a certain number

Instead, the networking that works best for me is the outcome of sincere, personal connections in which you get to know each other, get to know what you each do well, and get to know the clients you serve. Most importantly, these are the types of connections where you find ways to help each other, rather asking what they can do for you. While these connections may start over coffee or at a networking event, the conversation continues—through email, social media, or more face-to-face conversations.

Here is something that successful people know—and I didn't. It surprised me and may surprise you. The more successful the person, the more likely they are to ask what they can do for you. I remember the first time someone that I was in awe of asked me that

> The more successful the person, the more likely they are to ask what they can do for you.

question, and I was astounded. But then it happened again and again and again. And not only did they ask, but they followed through.

I've learned that networking is about offering more than you take. When you do this, the law of reciprocity kicks in. Every time you help someone, someone else appears to help you. Every time you are generous, a generosity comes your way. It's not a one-to-one equation, and it's not always from the same person, but over time, the assistance you provide others comes back to you tenfold.

Think of your network like money that earns compound interest. One connection leads to three more, and those three lead to six more—and on and on—until, before you know it, your life is filled with an amazing group of people whom you can help just as they will help you. You've created a group you can reach out to for help and advice, and a group you can support in ways only you can.

3. Know What Your Hourly Rate Really Is

I made this rookie mistake. I see others make it as well. As you are considering going independent, you hear that someone with similar skills is charging what seems like an astonishing rate, let's say $150 per hour. You are stunned. Then you do the math: $150 per hour x 40 hours per week x 48 weeks of a year = $288K per year. Wow, we'll be on easy street!

There are multiple fallacies in this logic. Let me share the main three that tripped me up.

First, not every single hour of your working day will be billable. Subcontractors might come closer to parity between their working day and billable hours since their agency's primary goal is to bill for as many hours as possible. If you land a long-term project (six months or more) where you will be utilized full time, you may get close over the course of that one project. But most freelancers who are balancing multiple engagements will not bill 100 percent of their available working hours. Instead, they will spend a certain percentage of their work time maintaining and developing the business— writing proposals, creating and updating their website, networking, and submitting bids on work.

Second, that $150 hourly rate is not the same as your net income from an employer. By the time your paycheck from your regular job lands in your bank account, several things have happened. Taxes have been both matched and deducted. Benefits have most likely been paid for, or at least a substantial portion of them. Money may have been deducted for retirement or charitable giving.

In contrast, your payment for services as an independent is a gross amount, not the net. That means the $150 per hour you get paid must include taxes, both state and federal, and any other benefits that are important to you: medical, dental, vision, retirement, and/or savings. This happens after you get paid, not before.

Finally, you are running a business, and running a business involves expenses. While our expenses tend to be far less than capital-intensive businesses, we still have them. A typical expense list includes a phone, a PC, software, office supplies, a website (and costs associated with that), marketing expenses, and travel.

A more realistic way to do the math on your services that would bill at $150 per hour is this: $150 per hour x 80 hours per month x 11 months = 132K in gross income. But you then have to subtract 25% for taxes and health care and another 15% for expenses. By my calculation, that means your net income is $84,150. Not bad, especially for all the reasons like freedom and control that come with this career—but a long way from $288K.

Providing independent professional services is a high margin / low investment business. But it is a business. Even with low investment needs and high margins, it is possible to run aground.

> Providing independent professional services is a high margin / low investment business. But it is a business. Even with low investment needs and high margins, it is possible to run aground.

4. Have a Clear and Compelling Value Proposition

As an employee, you have a resume that lists all you've done, where you've studied, and how wonderful you are.

As a consultant, that information is helpful, but an employer's question has shifted from "What have you done?" to "What can you do for me?"

Previous accomplishments become embellishments. The core message you need to craft is how your wonderful skills and accomplishments can help your client solve a problem or realize an opportunity. The greater your clarity, the more likely you are to be referred to others or called upon. The more your value proposition focuses on client value and what you can do for a client, the more likely you are to be hired. Simply stated, it is **NOT** about **YOU**. It is about **THEM**.

> The more your value proposition focuses on client value and what you can do for a client, the more likely you are to be hired. Simply stated, it is NOT about YOU. It is about THEM.

This is a difficult shift for many professionals to make. When asked what they do, they relate what they've done. When asked to tell about themselves, they regurgitate the jobs they've held, and the degrees they have amassed.

The core question independent consultants need to answer is: "How can I describe in a quantifiable way how my unique skills help clients solve a real problem or realize an opportunity?"

Some examples will help:

You are programmed to say this:	Say this instead:
I facilitate sales seminars.	I help companies increase their sales by an average of 5%.
I am a certified program manager.	I enable large projects to be delivered on time and under budget.
I develop online training courses.	I enable your employees to learn how to perform their jobs more effectively without the cost of traveling to a training class.
I do social media marketing.	I help retailers drive the right traffic to their websites, resulting in quantifiably higher sales.

The key here is to remember that you do have degrees and experiences and certifications and skills. But potential clients don't want to know what you've done in the past (except when they are validating your credentials). They want to know what you can help them to do differently or better or more of in the future.

Find Your Difference that Matters

Once you can clearly articulate the value you provide to clients, you will also need to be prepared to describe how you are different from others who provide similar services. What sets you apart from other program managers, sales trainers, or social media marketers? We're not talking about any old difference. You must have a difference that REALLY matters—to a client or potential client.

Perhaps you do social media marketing for retail companies that sell into the outdoor/adventure space. Perhaps your online training courses use state-of-the-art memory techniques that improve recall by 100 percent for learners. Perhaps you are really good at projects that require FDA oversight.

These things are compelling. They differentiate you. They enable you to stand out, and stand out in a way that matters to your clients.

I'm already feeling your resistance to this idea of narrowing what you offer. Think of it this way. I could provide services to retailers who are selling just about anything. I could design online learning modules where memory recall was nice but not necessary. I could manage just about any project. It's true. There are more potential clients if I offer multiple services across broader clients. But, it is also true that it is much harder to stand out in a crowded field or to offer higher-value services when you look just like everyone else.

Take it on faith here. Being bland and offering everything to everyone ensures that you will compete on the one variable that you don't want to—price.

Clients are more likely to hire the consultant who knows their unique problems and who can speak directly and clearly about their specific situations in ways that make a difference—to them.

5. Reskilling or Upskilling Is Up to You

By my calculations, my employer of 14 years most likely spent upwards of $100K on my development during my time at the company. They provided internal training, and they sent me to external training, where I learned additional skills and earned certifications. They paid for my MBA. All I had to do for these advantages was show up and be willing.

As an independent, I have an even greater need to develop and enhance my skill set while keeping old skills sharp. Clients demand that my skills are current and relevant. My market rate is higher with in-demand skills. My work improves as I improve. But, as an independent, my personal and professional skill development is up to me, which means I have to find the right opportunities and that I have to carve out time for development. It also means that I have to open my wallet and invest in myself.

Sometimes that investment is less about money and more about time. I'm swapping billable for non-billable hours. Sometimes that financial investment is huge—involving registration fees in the thousands and travel expenses. In fact, by my accounting, I've spent over $30,000 on my professional development since I started, and that does not count the books I've ordered (and studied), the webinars I've attended, and the coaching from peers and colleagues. I'm a careful spender, but I'm a spender. I view professional development as essential maintenance. The more I invest in myself, the better I am—the better my work, the higher my value, and the better clients I attract.

I'm always a bit taken aback when professionals who have the means are unwilling to invest several hundred dollars for coaching or a LEAP class. Of course, you can bumble along alone. Of course, you can find some free services. Of course, you can ask your neighbor for their advice. And, of course, you can save $500 in the short term.

Unfortunately, that approach may lose you the opportunity to earn a significant return on that $500. Look at it this way. A $500 professional development investment may allow you to raise your rates. In this case, not making the time or spending the money for additional training means you have forfeited potential income. Bottom line: Invest in yourself. You are the business.

6. Consulting Hours Are Different

Two things I did during my first year of consulting were especially eye-opening. The first was that most of the work I did was hourly, and so I had to keep meticulous records detailing my billable time and what I had accomplished. The second was that, in a quest to understand how to do this work, I tracked all the hours by categories (marketing, finances, networking, professional development, etc.).

My parents raised me to be honest and not to cheat anyone. Period. And so the hours I billed were the hours I worked—really worked. They did not include times when I thought about work or fiddled around trying to get focused. I only billed for heads down, crank it out work.

When I started, I tracked my time meticulously in two ways—tracking how I spent all my work hours and separately tracking billable hours and what I got accomplished. After reviewing both ways I tracked time, I had a huge revelation—my consulting hours were extremely productive. For most of my life as an employee, I had been putting in lots of hours but was not always very productive. As a consultant, I was amazed by how much I could get done with total focus and no distractions. It made me realize the amount of time and energy all those distractions took out of my workday.

For me, a consulting hour is a supercharged, productive hour, especially when I can block my time and give my complete focus to a task for a full hour or half a day. These hours are very different from the hours I spent as an employee, where distractions were continual, meetings were constant, and my focus was not as fine-tuned.

It is amazing how productive you can be when you peel off all the distractions and nonessentials. You find that sixty-hour work weeks are not required. You learn that your lack of focus was frittering away your ability to contribute and the ability to enjoy the rest of your life. You realize that the more focused you are, the higher your net hourly income is.

> It is amazing how productive you can be when you peel off all the distractions and nonessentials. You find that sixty-hour work weeks are not required. You learn that your lack of focus was frittering away your ability to contribute and the ability to enjoy the rest of your life. You realize that the more focused you are, the higher your net hourly income is.

7. You Can Grow Your Income Without Working More Hours

Okay—I may be a slow learner, but growing income without working more didn't seem like a possibility to me until it happened. I'd been working on my own for about five years when I started to see some things happening in my practice that enabled me to make more money for the same amount of effort.

The first thing I noticed as I gained experience, earned great references, and invested in my own skill development was that I could bill at higher rates. It was a pretty straightforward step, moving from $125 an hour to $150 to

$200 and eventually to $250. Cha-ching! If you do the math, upskilling and experience led to the benefit of a 100 percent raise. Far, far bigger than any raise I got in my job, even when I had earned a nice promotion.

The second was that, as my practice grew, I needed a team of people who met my standards and could deliver well for clients. I began to bring on subcontractors to work client engagements for me (I call them Practice Partners), which allowed me to make bigger sales and bill more hours. Remember that a downside of subcontracting your work is that the company that sold the work keeps a portion of the billable rate for their considerable time and trouble (and I'm not being funny—it is considerable, and every penny is earned).

The math of subcontracting works this way: I charge the client the market rate for your talent, deduct my markup, and you get the remainder. If your market rate is $100 per hour—that is what the client is billed. I might take 25 percent, so you make $75 per hour for the work you do with me as a subcontractor. Markups vary from 15 percent to 100 percent (which I think is unconscionable). Even with my lower markups (I tend to be in the 25 percent range), I can make bigger sales with a bigger team and charge for more than for my labor alone.

The third strategy was that I hired back-office help to take care of some office details and was able to pay them at a lower rate than my own hourly fee. For every hour that I could deliver on client work and someone else was doing the back-office work, I made more money. For example, if I paid my accountant $50 per hour and that freed me to do five more hours of client work per month at $150 per hour, I made $500 more dollars.

Fourth, I began to find ways to generate passive income. This could mean writing books, creating online courses, or licensing your content. I wrote a book with the primary goal of putting my ideas out there and building my reputation. As a secondary benefit, these concepts generated income, regular income. Income that I don't have to do anything more than notice that Amazon sent me a check this month. Now for me, this is not the "I'm rich, and so now I can retire" type of income. But for many, the ability to turn their expertise into products that they can monetize substantially increases their income.

8. You Can Shape/Sharpen Your Brand and Offerings

I can still recall how much angst I had in the first six months of going independent. I had to create a company name. I had to decide on a legal structure, select a logo, buy a URL, put up a website, and most importantly, define what exactly I was going to do to make a living all by myself.

I had a list of over 100 possible company names and then chose K. Taylor & Associates LLC. Boring, but it worked. I considered so many logos that my designer threw up his hands in disgust and began doodling on the computer, thereby creating my first logo, which served me well for six years. I began doing what I knew best: offering change management services and being a part of large project teams.

All of that introspection and playing around was truly needed and helpful. What was not needed was the stress I put myself through while making those decisions. I felt as if these were "life and death," forever decisions. They were not.

K. Taylor & Associates LLC is still my parent company, but I do business now as Evergreen Leadership. I have a new logo, and I'm on my fourth website overhaul. The leadership development work I do today has its roots in the work I started doing, but it is a different service offering. I've cofounded a second company, LEAP, which was not foreseeable at the start.

In reality, you really can't fully define something you've not experienced. Until you've worked with those first few clients, you can't possibly know what type of clients you work with best. Until you test your skills in the real world, it's tough to describe what you truly are brilliant at and what you never want to do again, ever! So just give it a go.

All this shows is that you just need to start. If you are waiting for the perfect name, logo, and service offering, you may never get off the ground. Know that you can change and adapt and continue to fine-tune who you are, what you offer, and how that is communicated to the world.

In reality, you really can't fully define something you've not experienced. Until you've worked with those first few clients, you can't possibly know what type of clients you work with best. Until you test your skills in the real world, it's tough to describe what you truly are brilliant at and what you never want to do again, ever! So just give it a go. And trust that over time, as you get smarter and better and have more experience, you can change and adapt and shape your independent practice to be the perfect fit for you.

9. It Can Be Lonely

As someone who hovers right on the line between introvert and extrovert, the mix of sometimes being with clients and sometimes working from my very quiet home office holds great appeal. Be forewarned that if you are high on extroversion, those home office days can be difficult, really difficult.

Many of my more extroverted peers find ways to overcome this "I just need to be around people" loneliness. Some lease a co-working space where they can work around others. Some use social media to connect with others. Most attend networking events, which can fill some of our need for human contact. But, as an independent, you need to know and plan for the fact that you will have a mix of client-facing days and home-alone days.

Whether you are an introvert or an extrovert, there is a different type of loneliness that challenges many independents. And that is the loneliness that comes from being a solopreneur and having the obligation to chart your own course, make your own decisions, and wrestle through tough client situations without a boss to go to for decision-making help or peers to go to for advice. It's easy to feel very alone as you face decisions that will shape your future and success going forward. It feels like a lot of pressure when you are standing by yourself and making big decisions. I learned in my second year of business that it didn't have to be as lonely as I was making it.

My friend and past business partner from eastern Pennsylvania, Carmen (remember her from my early days), referred me to someone in the Indianapolis area whom she thought would be a good connection. That person referred me to someone else. That second someone else was Kim Donahue, who encouraged me to meet her husband, Mike Donahue, who chaired a peer-to-peer network through an organization called Vistage.

I wasn't sure what to expect, but I joined his group and found an amazing resource. Every month, I would meet with other independents who were also building their businesses. We were in similar situations but were not competitors, so we helped each other. We discussed our challenges and successes, learned from each other's experiences, and supported each other through tough times. I still credit my early days in Mike's group as helping me get my business off to a good start by providing me with a rich and valuable network that encouraged me to think bigger and better.

There are many ways that others can be a part of your regular work routine to ease the loneliness and provide a sounding board. Here are a few ways I've overcome this loneliness:

- **Become an active part of a professional association.** You'll meet like-minded peers, build your network, stay abreast of your industry, and maybe even snag a client. The key word here is ACTIVE. Volunteer. Be on the board. Speak. Present. For the value here is not just rubbing shoulders with other humans at the monthly meeting but developing trusted relationships over time.

- **Join a mastermind group.** Until I was an entrepreneur, I didn't know these existed, but they do—and they can be transformative. The concept is simple: you meet with a group of individuals who have similar situations and goals as you. The group meets regularly to learn and share together. Each meeting is facilitated by an experienced professional, and you pay to be a part of a mastermind group. Shop around and ensure that the group you choose is aligned with your needs, which means the facilitator is solid and other group members are peers whose advice and counsel you would welcome.

- **Collaborate with other independents.** I'm able to deliver on bigger engagements because I have a wonderful network of Evergreen Leadership Practice Partners. These are peers who are willing to join me in providing services, project by project. Having my Practice Partners join me on a larger engagement provides the client with better service, enables all of us to learn from each other, and combats the loneliness of being the sole provider on an engagement. At other times, I'll be asked to collaborate with a trusted peer as a subcontractor for their engagement. No matter who is leading, being part of a professional team providing high value to a client is a peak consulting experience.

10. You are Not an Employee – Don't Act Like One

At this point, I've spent fourteen years on my own and fourteen years working at a big company. These experiences were different, very different. Don't confuse the two. As an employee, you look to your boss to set your direction and to focus your work. As an independent, you set your own priorities and have to determine how to reach them.

If you are the type of person who requires external mechanisms to get to work, to do your work, and to do your work on time, please stay employed. There are differences between an employee mindset and a consultant mindset. To succeed on your own, you have to love taking ownership and acting independently.

As an employee, external mechanisms keep you on track. Perhaps you have to report your time, or your boss expects you to be at work for the hours you are paid. You probably have specific objectives, deadlines, and productivity goals. As an independent, you can start your day as early or as late as you want. You can work as little or as much as you want. You can choose not to set deadlines, or you can choose to ignore deadlines.

As a salaried employee, you are paid a set amount every week. There are times during that week when you might kickback or waste time. There are other weeks (or months) when you put it on the line and go above and beyond with your time. There are times that you spend your time doing something that doesn't add much value. There are times you are less productive or when you just wait it out because others haven't gotten you what you need to do your part.

As an independent, you goof off on your own time, not on billable time. If you are not adding value, you don't bill for it. If you are waiting, you are off the clock. If you are less than productive, you adjust your rates to reflect that fact.

As an employee, you might whine about problems or complain about coworkers. As a consultant, your job is to come up with solutions and solve problems, not to complain about them. If there are true barriers or risks, you raise them. But not as complaints—as observations with some suggestions on mitigations.

As an employee, you might spend some time gossiping. As an independent, you are never going to put yourself in a position of being less than respectful to those you work with. You are not going to waste time and would never bill a customer for time you've slipped into junior high gossip behavior.

A Short Summary

In this chapter, I shared some "insider secrets"—things that I was neither aware of or that no one shared with me before I started my independent consultancy. Before you make the leap, it is helpful to know:

1. Client delivery is your first priority, but not your only one
2. Your network is an asset; treat it accordingly
3. What your hourly rate really is
4. A clear and compelling value proposition (and a difference that matters) is important
5. Reskilling or upskilling is up to you
6. Consulting hours are different
7. You can grow your income without working more hours
8. You can shape/sharpen your brand and offerings
9. It can be lonely
10. You are not an employee; don't act like one

What Does This Mean for You?

You've peeked behind the curtains a bit. I've shared some ups and downs and hard realities of being independent.

Take some time and think about:

➜ What in this chapter was a complete surprise to you?

➜ What excites you?

➜ What gives you pause?

CHAPTER 9

WHY WOULD ANYONE HIRE
A SMALL INDEPENDENT?

If you have read this far in the book, or even if you've jumped around, you will know two things. First, more and more organizations are using independents. Second, more and more professionals are choosing independent consulting or freelancing as a career. You might think these are acts of desperation by both sides—the pathetic professional who just lost a job or who is unemployed coupled with a leader who just can't keep good talent on the team they manage. I encourage you to rethink that assumption.

While there are instances of consulting in a job gap or the need for professional help in an emergency, these cases are increasingly becoming the outliers. The more common norm is that savvy professionals are choosing independence, and savvy leaders are choosing to work with independents as a strategic choice.

Earlier in the book, I detailed the many reasons why high-performing professionals were choosing independence. In this chapter, I'll help you understand and put words around why your potential clients would choose to work with you, rather than one of the Big Four consulting companies or a local agency.

Independents Have Talent They Need

I'll start with the most compelling: some of the best talent available is working independently. In order to be successful as an independent, one must not only have the skills to do the task well but must execute well enough to secure a referral or an invitation to do additional work.

I'll start with the most compelling: some of the best talent available is working independently. In order to be successful as an independent, one must not only have the skills to do the task well but must execute well enough to secure a referral or an invitation to do additional work. It may be (okay, it is) a bit Darwinian, but truly it is an environment where the top-notch professionals do well, and the others fold their tent and find a job.

Your potential client may be a midsized company with competent IT employees, but when the time comes to consider upgrading their core operating systems, an independent expert is going to bring enormous value. Perhaps your client has grown to the size that they need the services of a CFO or CMO or HR strategist but not on a full-time basis. You might find a client that wants to introduce a new capability to their organization, but they don't have the expertise on staff.

When clients hire independents, they are sourcing for more than just technical talent. In order to be successful, independent professionals bring skills broader than their specific technical skill set. Small independents are valuable assets who can simultaneously assess situations quickly, stay focused on results, and maintain good working relationships. They know how to communicate well, typically at all levels of the organization. They help the client's staff get better in the area they were hired for and help your organization move forward in significant ways. These capabilities make small independents competitive and compelling reasons for why other companies will hire you.

Independents Provide an Outside Perspective

Two of the greatest things you bring as an independent is objectivity about your client's situation coupled with a breadth of experience from other organizations. You can see things that your client, immersed up to their eyeballs in alligators, cannot. You can put things in perspective for them. You can offer ideas beyond the paltry few their staff can come up with. Your role is to assess and provide candid recommendations, something that those inside an organization might struggle with.

As a top-notch independent, you bring four specific dynamics with you that can help your client be more clearheaded about their situation and how to move forward.

1. **Independents have a broader perspective.** Independent professionals bring their broader expertise as an asset. They may have worked with multiple organizations before they began consulting. Once they began consulting, they experience a myriad of different companies, cultures, approaches, and situations. They bring the outside in, and that is a huge benefit.

2. **They have a specific expertise.** It may be coding or culture. It may be customer acquisition or tax codes. No matter—there is something that this person has expertise in. Often it is expertise that is lacking in the hiring organization, or that is needed for a short term project.

3. **They speak more freely.** Independent professionals are hired for their expert analysis, and they will provide it. Their job is to assess, to recommend, and then to implement solutions that solve the client's problem (and keep it solved). To do that, independents will share things with their clients straight up—as they see them.

4. **They are less emotional about the situation.** Making difficult decisions and changes within an organization can be hard. There are people involved: employees, customers, trusted vendors. People feel history and pride in all the ways work is done now. There are blinders, as "how we do it here" becomes cemented into the culture. An independent consultant brings a less emotional perspective. This does not mean they don't care. It just means they have less baggage attached to the status quo and less trepidation about how changes will affect themselves or others. This enables them to bring more objectivity than internal staff typically can.

5. **They are vested fully in your success.** All the independents I know really want to make a positive difference for their clients and their organizations. They want projects to succeed, sales to soar, and employees to thrive. There are three factors that lead to this: 1) they are doing work that they are really good at and, in most cases, passionate about; 2) their success is linked to their clients, and they cannot survive as an independent doing mediocre work; and 3) they have a strong desire to serve and to make a difference.

Independents Bring Up-to-Date Skills and Knowledge

Keeping up with current technology, innovations, and best practices is difficult, no matter what the area of specialty. Independents can provide needed expertise to an organization without making a hire. This can work especially well when the skill set needed is more cutting edge, and employees have not been exposed to or equipped with the new skills, methods, or tools. It can also work well when a client needs a certain skill set for a fixed point in time. For example, they may need help coding or customizing some software, but once that is done, they have no long-term need for those specific skills. In that case, it makes perfect sense to hire in what you need when you need it.

If it is a capability needed over time, an independent can put in place the initial build or framework, train your employees, and then support them. Contrast this with the time, money, and effort of finding an employee with the right skills to hire and then putting in the time and effort required to orient and onboard them, all before they can put a new practice into place and do the work of skilling up your team. An independent arrives ready to go. They can help you get a solid start and train your employees so that they can stand alone.

Here is the key question for clients considering an independent: "Do I need this skill or expertise over time?" If the answer is yes, then make sure that part of the independent's role involves training and equipping your folks with the information they need to know. Beware of independents who guard their knowledge and are reluctant to help others do what they can do. My mantra is always to equip my client partners with the higher-level skills in the area I'm helping them with. Client independence is the goal, not client dependence.

Independents Are Hired for Just the Right Amount of Time

There is some work in organizations that needs to be done every single day, year in, and year out. Such work often requires specific expertise in the organization, and it is the core of "what they do." Filling these roles with a W-2 employee (either part- or full-time) is a perfect choice.

There will be some other work that is shorter in duration. Work that will take a few months rather than a few years. Work like this is typically a one-time need or part of a limited duration project. This is a great place to utilize independent talent.

It makes good sense to hire a customer service manager and staff. It makes equally good sense to hire a contracted professional to help implement a new CRM. It makes great sense to have a full-time building engineer, and it also makes great sense to use an independent to support a building engineer to perform an energy audit and identify ways to make a building greener and more sustainable.

Independent consultants can work as few as a couple of days or as long as a few years (if assigned to a longer-term project) and everything in between. If hiring for a more long-term assignment, be certain to work with the HR function to assure good standing with employment laws that differentiate between W-2 and 1099 employees.

Independents Can Get You to a Quicker Start

Even when it goes lickety-split, hiring needed regular employee talent can take months—many months. The hiring manager needs to get approval, the job needs to be posted, and then the wait begins. And once applicants have been identified, there is the interviewing and the vetting, then the offer. Then the two to four weeks to give notice before beginning. And even then, it takes a few weeks (or months) to get the new employee onboarded, oriented, and productive. All this time is well spent to find the right hire for a longer-term role.

Contrast that with hiring an independent, which can happen much more quickly. It may take weeks, but seldom months. There is still a search and vetting, but the search is more targeted, and independents typically respond quickly. If they are available, they will also be able to start quickly.

Even better, once there is an established relationship (typically with a master contract and other procurement requirements in place), it's relatively easy to bring that consultant who works well with a particular client onboard for other projects. These independents are trusted. They work effectively with their clients, and they know the organization and how to get work done. I've often gotten big projects started with my repeat customers in a matter of a week or two—and when time is critical, this is a real advantage.

Smaller Firms May Offer More Value

To end this chapter, I'm going to put in an unabashed plug for small independents and midsize consulting firms. While we may not have the cache of an Accenture or Deloitte or KPMG, we bring value in different ways.

I've seen the talent that the big firms bring to an engagement. Their top talent is reserved for making the sale and interacting with executives. Their "feet on the street" talent is more junior. While these junior folks are smart and driven, they are less experienced. Contrast that to an engagement with a smaller firm where, more than likely, you get to work with the principal or a very experienced team.

The top name firms also charge top dollar for their services because they have much more overhead. They have hired exceptionally bright junior talent, and they pay really well for the work they do. They also have a reputation to support, and high prices are a way to validate it. Finally, they charge robust rates just because they can.

Smaller or midsize independents are not going to be inexpensive, but they will come in at a price point below the Big Four. This is typically because they don't have the same overhead demands and are usually working with a mix of firms, including some that would never consider the prices a Big Four firm command.

And finally, in a larger metro area, there will be really good talent nearby. Eliminating or reducing travel expenses can decrease costs by thousands per week (perhaps tens of thousands per week if there is an entire team of consultants). Lower travel expenses should not be the primary reason to pick a small independent, but it could be another reason that independents and small-size consultancies might be the best bet for many clients (assuming talent is the same or even better).

A Short Summary

In this chapter, I shared many reasons that organizations benefit from working with small or mid-sized independent consultants. Here they are:

1. Independents have the needed talent

2. They provide an outside perspective

3. They bring up-to-date skills and knowledge

4. You can hire them for just the right amount of time

5. They can get things off to a quicker start

6. They can offer more value

What Does This Mean for You?

➡ What advantages do you bring to a client who is considering engaging with you?

➡ How are you different in ways that matter from the top consulting firms in your area of expertise?

➡ How would you respond to a client considering your services against those of a bigger firm?

CHAPTER 10

YOU MAY BE YOUR BIGGEST OBSTACLE

You've gotten to this point in the book. You're intrigued by the notion of owning your own career. There is something that happens to us as humans when we dream of doing something big. We get scared. And that little voice in our head begins to chatter at us.

It is incessant and may be telling you that this is not the time. It may reassure you that you'll do this big thing sometime, but other things need to come first. You may tell yourself that you'll do this but just not right now. You'll do it later when you:

- Have more money in the bank

- Have your kids through college

- Work ten more years, retire, and then do what you love

- Aren't quite so busy with so many other things

- Get one more certification, go to one more class, learn one more thing...

Some of these reasons are legit. If you are living paycheck to paycheck, your first task is to get your finances in order. If you are within a short grasp

> Far too often, when we are failing to make progress in a goal we've set or a vision we are bringing to life, most often the enemy is within.

of a pension (perhaps one year, but not ten years), take the longer view. If your life is in chaos, it's best to get a few things in order.

Far too often, when we are failing to make progress in a goal we've set or a vision we are bringing to life, most often the enemy is within. It is our own fear that causes us to freeze. It is resistance to what might be; what we might create; or how we might dare to do something big and meaningful.

Those fears show up when your internal dialog is saying things like:

- Who am I to do this big thing?

- Am I really good enough?

- Would anyone really hire little old me?

- Better to slog through the known than to risk the unknown

People who create (like authors, entrepreneurs, new product designers, or anyone with the desire to bring something new into the world) have a term for this voice in our heads that holds us back, that encourages us to give up our dreams by pulling us firmly back into the status quo—we call it resistance (Pressfield 2002).

Resistance Is Really Fear in Different Forms

Resistance is probably with us due to our genetic wiring and evolutionary inheritance. It is human nature to be cautious when things are changing. We are hyperalert in new situations, new roles, and new locations, and for good reason. In the past, new could very easily be a predator ready to make you his midday meal or an environmental risk that posed a hazard.

Yet our fear of new things persists even though we are not in mortal danger, and often, it can paralyze us. The challenge is to sort out the fears that we should be paying attention to (like shifting markets, red numbers in our bank accounts, or obsolete skill sets), and the ones we need to bring to the surface, examine, and summarily dismiss. The reality is that fear holds us back all the time, and the majority of that time, the fear is either unwarranted or has a low likelihood of materializing.

The hard truth is that the bigger the "thing," the greater the fear. Starting your very own professional independent career is a BIG thing, and you will have fears.

The question is: will you choose to overcome those fears or choose to stay where you are, doing what you are doing? For me, staying in place was a far bigger risk than the risk of stepping out.

Only you can weigh the risks and rewards. Only you can find ways to overcome or mitigate the risks. And only you can decide what you want to do with your life.

What Are We Afraid Of?

Examined by the light of day, some of our fears are downright ridiculous. Others are dim possibilities. And a few may be legitimate. Identifying the fears that you hold and then managing them is easier if you know what to look for.

Here is a list of common fears (at least common to me)—and some thoughts on how to overcome them.

- **Fear of Failure**

    Face it. You will have failures. There are no perfect consultants, engagements, or practices. Some engagements will fail because of factors you could not control. Others will fail because you missed something critical. Maybe you misjudged timing, readiness, or got distracted. The goal is not to be failure free but to spot that swampy territory that comes just before you are about to fail and to take action quickly to

> Face it. You will have failures. There are no perfect consultants, engagements, or practices.

avert disaster. Each failure will teach you something if you allow it to. Each failure will build your skills, your resilience, your empathy, and your internal GPS.

It's not that I'm advocating big messy failures. I'm just stating the simple fact that when you stretch and do challenging things, you will not do them perfectly 100 percent of the time. You will look back and wonder how you could have been that stupid or misguided. But you'll be smarter and more valuable and a better person because of it. Caveat: that is only if you pick yourself up, learn what you can, and keep pressing forward.

The best way to overcome this fear is just to acknowledge it exists. You won't execute perfectly. There are things you don't know quite yet. You'll do some things brilliantly and some things not so much. Knowing, deep inside, that you'll be able to manage, make amends, and come out all right in the end will make you better.

- **Fear of Rejection**

This is THE big fear in the selling process, and the most common fear I hear others articulate. You know that as you pitch a project, submit a proposal, or respond to an RFP that others are doing the same thing for that coveted work you want. You won't bat 1,000 (and, if you do, I want to know how). The question then becomes—is it fear of rejection or fear of competition? Rejection smacks of the personal—they just didn't like, honor, or respect you. Competition connotes selecting the best fit and is combined with the knowledge that you win some and you lose some. That is how the game is played.

I ask you to consider (and then to mitigate) another manifestation of the fear of rejection. This one happens after you've been selected for an engagement and, in my experience, is far more common. What happens is that you've started an engagement only to have the employees in the client organization reject your work, your process, and/or your methodology.

Even when you meet with a willing audience, it is not always a motivated audience. Other things are competing for their time and attention. They too are afraid to try this new thing advocated by you, this unknown or outside person. This situation, of course, takes you smack dab back to that fear of failure. You've been engaged to do this big thing with the client, and you see, before your very eyes, the silence, the lack of energy and focus, and the pall of lack of commitment. The good news is that there are some really good strategies and tactics to avoid this place (one of the positive outcomes of my change management expertise). Even better, they are things you can learn and do.

- **Fear of Scarcity**

This is the fear that there is just not enough work to go around or that you are not smart enough, motivated enough, or well-connected enough to make this successful. The opposite of fear of scarcity is an attitude of abundance, in which you believe there is plenty of work for all, that you are abundantly able to do this work, and that you have all you need.

True story: I was in the period between declaring my intention to leave my employer and actually launching my practice. I can still recall my eager anticipation as I arrived at a local meeting of the training professional association where I was excited to announce my big news. It was a small gathering, and we went around the table with each person "checking in." Just before my turn, one of my respected peers eagerly announced that she was launching her new training firm. She had her business set up, had a name, a logo, and a first client. I was shocked and stunned. When it came to my turn, I stammered about doing the same thing as she was and apologized that, just yet, I had neither a name nor logo (and no need to talk about the client thing). I slunk out of the meeting, defeated and concerned. I could not imagine that clients would ever work with me instead of my peer. I came dangerously close to throwing in the towel, even before I had really started.

Nonetheless, I was fortunate enough to keep going. And, as things turned out, this peer found that consulting was not for her at this particular time in her life, and after a short time, she returned to her job as an employee. She does great work, and that was a good decision for her. I am eternally grateful that I didn't react to my scarcity panic.

- **Fear of Brilliance**

This one is going to sound absurd. Brilliance? Fear of my own brilliance? Believe me—it is real. The more I get to know really successful professionals, the more I realize that this is a very common fear. There are those things that we do with our own unique signature strengths, the places where we shine. These are the places that can scare us the most.

Some call it the imposter syndrome, or the belief that others are going to find out that you are not really as good as you appear to be. Some believe in the notion that "work is work" and what you shine at does not feel like work, so it cannot be real. Others feel like doing what we do best has a show-off quality or is not very equal. Others are so focused on their flaws that they cannot see their brilliance.

Marianne Williamson sums it up best in this statement:

> Our deepest fear is not that we are inadequate. Our deepest fear is that we are powerful beyond measure. It is our light, not our darkness that most frightens us. We ask ourselves, Who am I to be brilliant, gorgeous, talented, fabulous? Actually, who are you not to be? You are a child of God. Your playing small does not serve the world. There is nothing enlightened about shrinking so that other people won't feel insecure around you. We are all meant to shine, as children do. We were born to make manifest the glory of God that is within us. It's not just in some of us; it's in everyone. And as we let our own light shine, we unconsciously give other people permission to do the same. As we are liberated from our own fear, our presence automatically liberates others (Williamson 1992).

- **Fear of Success**

  Fear of success is a bit different than the fear of brilliance. To overcome a fear of brilliance is to accept your gifts, talents, and strengths and to own, totally, who you are. To overcome a fear of success, you must deem yourself worthy, and assure yourself that the change will be positive and that you'll not lose yourself in the process.

  We fear success for a variety of reasons. It means change. It means we have different but bigger challenges. We will leave some people behind. We may not be able to handle it. We may not be worthy. It may change us for the worse.

135

I believe that a fear of success comes from not having a clear, personal description of what success is for you. If you define success on a personal level, what is there to fear? If your definition includes adequate time for yourself, friends, and family—go for it. If it is about income level or lifestyle, know where you are aiming.

Overcoming Resistance

Doing something big always scares me. It will scare you. It scares just about everyone I know.

When I find myself stalling, rationalizing, and stuck, I have to recognize that it is my own, internal, self-created resistance that is holding me back.

Resistance takes many shapes yet is invisible and totally within. We blame others; we procrastinate; we have many reasons to yield to its power. The good news is that our resistance can be beaten. We can do that big thing. We can launch our own practices. We can reclaim our lives. We can offer the world our unique talents and skills.

How can you overcome your own resistance? In my experience, resistance fades when these things happen:

I take action. Even little steps make a difference. Try to move forward a bit every single day until momentum begins to build. I trust that I don't have to have the entire plan pulled together. I know that the first steps are exploratory. But I deeply know the importance of those first steps, that beget other steps and mark a sincere desire to create this thing.

I live in "how to" instead of "why not." I focus on what I do have and not where I am void. I focus on why this is important to me, those around me, and the greater world. I envision. I acknowledge the barriers and then either remove them or find a way around them. I spend my energy moving forward rather than looking back or spinning in all the reasons I should not begin.

I announce my intentions to the world. There is no greater accountability than saying what you want to do, out loud, to those who will support you, encourage you, and check on your progress. The wonderful thing is that once you do, help materializes and often from unexpected places.

I seek help from those who have gone before. Even a big "do it yourself-er" like me has learned that the path is shorter, the travails less troublesome, and the journey more joyful with a teacher or coach by your side.

A Short Summary

Many talented people are tripped up by their own fears or insecurities. We tell ourselves we will do this big thing sometime, just not now. This is called resistance.

Resistance is just fear, and it can show up in these ways:

- Fear of failure
- Fear of rejection
- Fear of scarcity
- Fear of brilliance
- Fear of success

When you experience resistance, you can do these things:

- Take action
- Ask "how to" rather than "why not"
- Announce your intention to the world
- Get help from those who have gone before

What Does This Mean for You?

➜ What fears surface for you when you contemplate being an independent professional?

➜ What fears are not worthy of your time, energy, and attention?

➜ What fears do you need to address by taking steps to avert or mitigate the perceived danger?

➜ When you have done something big in the past, what did you do to overcome resistance?

CHAPTER 11

GETTING STARTED

How to Know When to Go Independent

The path to owning your own independent career as a professional is as varied as the people who pursue this career choice. Remember our stories? Rhett worked for 37 years and then went independent. Katie started as an independent immediately after college. While many independents follow the path of working for an employer for a considerable amount of time and then utilizing that experience to go out on their own, there is an increasing trend of professionals going directly into consulting. It used to be that more senior folks chose independence, often in the last decade of their careers. Now millennial males are the fastest growing segment of independents (Manyika et al. 2011).

The answer to this is ambiguous, varied, and deeply personal. Your life circumstances may propel you into independence or may contribute to your choice to stay with a regular paycheck for a few more years. You may have to get things in order before you begin—obtain verifiable credentials, improve your network, or establish a financial safety net. You may conclude that independence is not for you, which is a sound decision for many.

If you are serious about getting started, no matter your timeline, this chapter outlines some good first steps.

Enter with Realistic Optimism

Launching and growing an independent consulting practice is hard. In fact, it is harder than you think. It will take longer than you ever imagined. You will be discouraged. You will face periods of doubt. You will long for a regular job and a steady paycheck. You will ask why, on God's green earth, did you decide to pursue a career in which putting yourself on the line and facing rejection after rejection was a part of the process?

Banish any illusions that may be dancing in your mind that you will be an instant success. Odds are that you won't. Forget any notions that it will be easier for you than for others, because it won't.

> Remember that anything big, anything important, anything transformational requires effort and lots of it. This is especially true when going independent. But also keep in mind that the rewards are worth the struggle. Period.

Remember that anything big, anything important, anything transformational requires effort and lots of it. This is especially true when going independent. But also keep in mind that the rewards are worth the struggle. Period.

For myself and for many others, the first few years are the toughest. Some are fortunate enough to land a client early on; others may have to show up, day after day, month after month before getting a tenuous toehold. During this time, you learn that the batting stats for selling work is one hit for every ten pitches. You will get used to the reality that you'll get more no's than yes's.

Early on, you are likely to spend up to 100 percent of your time seeking work and precious little time delivering it. Once you do land one of those first clients, you'll spend even more time putting the basics in place: the letters of engagements, the NDAs, the contracts, your processes and presentations, and your tools.

Then, once you have those first clients, you will quickly discover that there is, indeed, work you can do but don't want to do. There are clients you really don't want to work with and some types of work that you just don't want to do.

In those times, remember this: **Stay with it, and it will begin to flip.** You'll get processes and forms and infrastructure in place, so the next engagement takes less upfront effort. Do good work, and you'll get repeat business or referrals, which enable you to land the next gig much more easily. Word spreads, and people begin to know your work.

It may take two years to flip or three or even five. In those years, you continue to do the work. You find the work, and then do it to the best of your ability. You cultivate your network. You give back to your professional network.

And then the magic happens: Instead of you searching for the work, the work begins to find you. If you've been smart about it, the right work and the right clients at the right time show up on your doorstep. To others, it seems like this was easy, or you were lucky. But you know differently. You know it is because you've done the work of sticking it out through those lonely first years. You've proven yourself. Your reputation precedes you. And now, your job is to keep the magic happening—by showing up, by doing good work, by sharpening your skills, and by continuing to build your network.

Define What Success Is for You

One of the first things I did back in 2004 was write down what success meant for me—success both personally and as a business owner. I still refer back to those six paragraphs written over 15 years ago.

I review them to test that they are still accurate. Year after year, I find that they are. I review them to align my day-to-day actions with my larger vision for my practice and my life. When I've strayed, I course correct. I review them to remind myself how grateful I am for the opportunities I've had, for the choices I've made, and for the work that I've done. Because for me, it has led me to a career and a life that feels just perfect for me.

As you do this exercise, know that success can look like many different things for many different people. For some, it may be the type of work they are doing. For others, success comes from the acclaim they receive for their work. For others, it may be the financial rewards or the way you spend your time or way you feel at the end of a day at work.

Put Together a Plan

As the proverb from a fortune cookie says, "Many a false step was made by standing still." It's time to take action. You've put on paper the place you would like to be. To get to that place of success will require some work. And to do the right work that will lead you to the right place, you will need a plan.

Do not listen to those well-intentioned individuals who advise you to put together a 40- to 60-page business plan. You only need a traditional business plan if you are going to get funding for start-up money or loans. You are not—so don't waste time or effort on creating a traditional business plan.

But, you should have a plan that gives you direction and focus. Your plan may be a 60-day or six-year plan. If you are on the six-year runway, your plan will be more strategic and directional. Look over the preceding chapters and see where you have gaps that need to be closed, perhaps it involves building a financial safety net or a more robust network. It may be that you want to obtain a certification or build out a portfolio of your work. In any case, whether for 60 days or six years, have a plan. And even more importantly, work the plan.

If you are launching soon, your plan is going to be more detailed and tactical. At LEAP, we've created a ten-step checklist for getting started, which you can access at LeapRightNow.biz

Find Support

One of the most valuable things you can do is to get help and support. There is no doubt that you can bumble through this by yourself. I did. Many others have. But what I learned over time is that when I worked with others to learn more about running a business, my business went to the next level.

There was so much about launching and growing a professional consulting practice that I didn't know, and others helped me learn. I joined mastermind classes. I hired coaches. I read about this business, and I kept learning, because the smarter I am, the better my business becomes.

This is not the time for false bravado or toughing it out on your own. It is time to reach out to others. I believe that you'll find, as I did, that successful people everywhere are willing to share, mentor, teach, and support.

This journey is not for the faint of heart. It can be challenging and perplexing, but as with any journey, the load is lighter, and the travel more fun when it is shared.

A Short Summary

Starting an independent consulting practice takes time and effort, as does about anything else you do in this life that is important. Before you start, I encourage you to:

- Enter with realistic optimism (this book has helped you do that)
- Create your own personal definition of success to guide you
- Put together a plan
- Find support

What Does This Mean for You?

Envision your best life and career five years from now.

➜ What are you doing?

➜ How do you spend your days?

➜ What type of work are you doing?

➜ Who are you working with?

➜ What type of income are you earning?

➜ How do your work and the rest of your life fit together?

Now that you've envisioned a future, consider three steps you can take to make your vision a reality:

➡ What can you do in the next 24 hours?

➡ What will you do in the next week?

➡ What do you need to do in the next 30 days to be happy with the progress you've made?

CHAPTER 12

YOU CAN DO THIS! WE CAN HELP

There are times in this world when we stumble into something that we give to others and also fills us up along the way. This is how I feel about the work we are doing at LEAP.

I first met Katie, the cofounder of LEAP, when I helped her transition from college graduate to successful independent professional. I offered my coaching and support because I saw her potential, knew she would do the work well, and liked her. What I didn't expect or see coming was how much joy I derived from helping her get her practice started.

I began to see how the career I had carved out looked very different than many of my peers. By taking the big step to "own my career," I was doing something that I loved. It was something I was good at, and it provided me with a good income. It also allowed me to balance my work and life in wonderful ways.

As we worked together, I began to realize that I had something of value that other professionals who were making "the leap" could benefit from. What I had learned over time (and rather haphazardly) could be organized, consolidated, and shared in a more systematic way to help others learn more quickly and easily.

So, even though I had no intention of beginning another company, LEAP was formed. I asked Katie to join me, because she brings skills in marketing, social media, and sales that are a must-have for small independents.

The more professionals we help, the more convinced I am of the value of this work. These experiences have shown me that we can help other skilled professionals realize the benefits of being independent. I hope this book has helped you along that journey.

I hope that you "own" whatever career path you choose and that it serves you well. And I hope that if you found value in this book, that you explore how Katie and I can help you launch and grow your independent professional career.

May you be blessed with meaningful work that enables you to use your talents and gifts in the service of others.

THANK YOU

Time is precious—especially in today's hyper-connected and fast-paced world. As such, I want to thank you for the time you've spent allowing me to share my thoughts on how you might own your career.

Also, thank yourself. The time you've spent thinking about taking control of your life and your career is vitally important. No matter whether you anticipate working for another five or fifty years, the time you've invested in yourself and your career by reading this book and doing the exercises will provide big dividends.

I'd love to hear your thoughts about the book and especially what it has sparked in you. If you have ideas on related topics that would be helpful, please share!

It is my sincere hope that your career, no matter what path(s) you choose, brings you the joy of doing the work you do best, the satisfaction of using your talents for something bigger than yourself, and the ability to integrate your life's work into your life.

Kris Taylor

LeapRightNow.biz
EvergreenLeadership.com
Explore@LeapRightNow.biz
LinkedIn.com/in/TaylorKris

Ready to Take the **LEAP?**

Learn how to claim your free copy of the LEAP Business 101 Checklist: 10 Things to Do to Start Your Own Consulting Business at

bit.ly/Owning-It

LEAP helps you launch and boost your consulting business through personalized programs that will fit you no matter where you are in your consulting journey.

Learn more about **LEAP** programs and a special **Owning It** discount for readers of this book at

LeapRightNow.biz/Owning-It-Special-Offer

Follow along with the latest updates from
LEAP, Kris, and Katie below:

Facebook: Facebook.com/LeapRightNow/

LinkedIn: LinkedIn.com/company/Leap-Right-Now

Website: LeapRightNow.biz

ABOUT THE AUTHOR

Kris Taylor is the founder of Evergreen Leadership (EvergreenLeadership. com) and cofounder of LEAP (LeapRightNow.biz). Her many years of work experience are rich in variety. She worked for ten years in education and nonprofit fields before making a career change to RR Donnelley, a Fortune 200 company. During her 14-year tenure at RR Donnelley, she fulfilled a variety of roles in departments ranging from human resources and operations to a corporate position in learning and development.

In 2004, Kris went out on her own and has been a successful independent consultant consistently, earning over $100K per year. Her initial consulting endeavor partnered with clients to create customized leadership development programs and was rebranded in 2011 as Evergreen Leadership. Her firm specializes in fostering skills in agility, collaboration, relationship building, accountability, and creativity. She writes, speaks, teaches, and coaches leaders at all levels, from C-suite to high-potential emerging leaders. In total, Kris has worked with over 60 organizations, from small entrepreneurial firms to Fortune 100 organizations.

Kris has also been on the faculty of Purdue's Certificate Program in Entrepreneurship and Innovation where she developed and taught a course on consulting and a course entitled Your Entrepreneurial Career. It was there that she met Katie McNamee. She so enjoyed helping Katie start her independent consulting firm, Elevate Online, that they decided to share what they had learned with others. They cofounded LEAP together in 2017 to coach other professionals considering, launching, or growing small independent consulting practices by providing practical guidance and support through coaching services and learning programs.

Kris is the author of *The Leader's Guide to Turbulent Times: A Practical, Easy-to-Use Guide to Leading in Today's Times.* She earned her undergraduate degree at West Virginia University and an MBA from Krannert Business School at Purdue University.

BIBLIOGRAPHY

Alleyne, Richard. "Welcome to the information age – 174 newspapers a day." *The Telegraph.* February 11, 2011. https://www.telegraph.co.uk/news/science/science-news/8316534/Welcome-to-the-information-age-174-newspapers-a-day.html.

Bernassani, Sophia. "10 Jobs Artificial Intelligence Will Replace (and 10 That Are Safe)." *Hubspot Blog.* July 2017. https://blog.hubspot.com/marketing/jobs-artificial-intelligence-will-replace .

Browne, Ryan. "70% of People Globally Work Remotely at Least Once a Week, Study Says." *CNBC Make It.* May 30, 2018. https://www.cnbc.com/2018/05/30/70-percent-of-people-globally-work-remotely-at-least-once-a-week-iwg-study.html.

Davis, Clark. "Downsizing Becomes Normal: Current Events in Historical Perspective." Origins. April 15, 1998. http://origins.osu.edu/history-news/downsizing-becomes-normal.

"Freelancing in America: 2018 Survey." UpWork. https://www.upwork.com/i/freelancing-in-america/2018/.

Gerber, Michael. *The E-Myth Revisited: Why Most Small Businesses Don't Work and What to Do About It.* New York: Harper Collins, 2004.

GreenTarget. "2017 Management Consulting Outlook." *GreenTarget* 2017.

Hyman, Louis. *Temp: How American Work, American Business, and the American Dream Became Temporary.* New York, NY: Viking, 2018.

Lesonsky, Rieva. "The State of Freelancing in America." SCORE. July 1, 2019. https://www.score.org/blog/state-of-freelancing-in-america.

Manyika, James, Susan Lund, Byron Auguste, Lenny Mendonca, Tim Welsh, and Sreenivas Ramaswamy. An Economy That Works: Job Creation and America's Future." McKinsey & Company, June 2011. https://www.mckinsey.com/featured-insights/employment-and-growth/an-economy-that-works-for-us-job-creation.

Marr, Bernard. "How Much Data Do We Create Every Day? The Mind-Blowing Stats Everyone Should Read." *Forbes*. May 21, 2018. https://www.forbes.com/sites/bernardmarr/2018/05/21/how-much-data-do-we-create-every-day-the-mind-blowing-stats-everyone-should-read/#7ff1e51a60ba.

Miller, Jody Greenstone, and Matt Miller. "The Rise of the Supertemp." *Harvard Business Review*. May 2012. https://hbr.org/2012/05/the-rise-of-the-supertemp.

Paynter, Ben. "The 10 Best Jobs of the Future." Popular Science.September 21, 2010. https://www.popsci.com/science/article/2010-08/10-best-jobs-future-0/.

Pink, Daniel. *Drive: the Surprising Truth about what Motivates Us.* New York: Riverhead Books, 2009.

Pofeldt, Elaine. "Are We Ready For A Workforce That Is 50% Freelance." *Forbes*. October 31, 2017. https://www.forbes.com/sites/elainepofeldt/2017/10/17/are-we-ready-for-a-workforce-that-is-50-freelance/.

Powers, Anna. "A Study Finds That Diverse Companies Produce 19% More Revenue." *Forbes*. June 28, 2018. https://www.forbes.com/sites/annapowers/2018/06/27/a-study-finds-that-diverse-companies-produce-19-more-revenue/#1aa2e8a0506f.

Pressfield, Steven. *The War of Art: Break Through the Blocks and Win Your Inner Creative Battles.* New York: Black Irish Entertainment, LLC 2002.

Rainie, Lee. "10 Facts About Jobs in the Future." Pew Research Center: Internet, Science & Tech. October 10, 2017. https://www.pewinternet.org/2017/10/10/10-facts-about-jobs-in-the-future/.

SBA. "Do economic or industry factors affect business survival? " SBA. June 2012. https://www.sba.gov/sites/default/files/Business-Survival.pdf.

Sieber, Chris. "Is Boutique Consulting Right for You?" *BetaVault*. March 31, 2009. https://www.vault.com/blogs/consult-this-consulting-careers-news-and-views/is-boutique-consulting-right-for-you.

Williamson, Marianne. *A Return to Love.* New York: Harper Collins, 1992.

Made in the USA
Lexington, KY
23 October 2019